The Primary
Physical Education
Handbook

Second edition

Jim Hall

A&C Black • London

First published 1999 by
A & C Black Publishers Ltd
37 Soho Square, London W1D 3QZ
www.acblack.com

Second edition 2004

Reprinted digitally 2003

ISBN 0 7136 6829 6

A CIP catalogue record for this book
is available from the British Library.

Cover illustration by Eleanor King

Cover design by James Watson

Note: Whilst every effort has been made to ensure that the content of this book
is as technically accurate as possible, neither the author nor the publishers can
accept responsibility for any injury or loss sustained as a result of the use of this material.

A & C Black uses paper produced with elemental chlorine-free pulp,
harvested from managed sustainable forests.

Printed and bound in Great Britain by CPI Bath.

Contents

Introduction

Good lesson plans and a sense of staff unity regarding the 'Why?', 'What?', and 'How?' of Physical Education, are essential contributors to a successful whole school programme with high standards and continuity from year to year. Included in this book are sample lesson plans and material designed to help with the 'Why?', 'What?' and 'How?'

Working in a hall or playground with apparatus, equipment, wide spaces, rapidly moving pupils, and behaviour and safety considerations to manage, is a problem, particularly for teachers with limited training in teaching Physical Education. This book aims to help teachers by providing information, ideas and practical help with planning, teaching and developing their Games, Gymnastic Activities and Dance lessons. It also aims to provide schools with suggestions for planning the content of their progressive programmes in the three activities, from Reception Year to Year 6.

The stimulation of almost non-stop, vigorous and enjoyable activity should be the most important feature and aim of Physical Education, ideally inspired by enthusiastic teachers who value the subject.

Jim Hall

For whole school success, there must be a sense of unity among all who teach the Physical Education programme. Staff should be in agreement about:

- what they teach
- why they teach it
- how they teach it.

The attitude of staff to what is 'good' about good Physical Education; to teaching methods; and to expectations for behaviour, standards and levels of achievement, needs to be agreed to ensure year to year continuity.

Ideally, the expressions of intent known as 'Aims' represent the combined views of the staff. If teachers limit the number of aims and concentrate on one main aim for half a term, they can achieve the changes they want to bring about in the ability, knowledge, understanding and attitudes of their pupils more easily.

Aim 1 *Inspire vigorous physical activity to promote normal healthy growth, suppleness and strength.*

Remember that you are, first and foremost, purveyors of action. Let your lessons be scenes of busy activity. Put the 'physical' into Physical Education.

Let all lessons have one thing in common – near continuous and enjoyable action, expressed in deep breathing, perspiration and smiling faces. Teachers must avoid 'dead spots' in lessons, when nothing is happening, in the following ways.

- Ensure punctual starts so that the whole lesson plan is covered.
- Encourage good behaviour to prevent interruptions.
- Teach and coach while the class is working, rather than having lots of stoppages for demonstrations.
- Beware of inactive queues in apparatus work by providing lots of return activities. Avoid games inaction by using small-sided teams of 2–5 players.
- Develop a 'Be found working, not waiting' understanding by all to maintain the action and the learning of the skills.
- Ask the class to concentrate on one main feature. For example, 'Feel your heels and knees lifting,' as they run, rather than the time-consuming and confusing 'Lift your heels; lift your knees; lift your head; swing your arms straight forward and back; change direction somewhere; look for spaces to run into.'

Physical Education is most valuable when the participation is enthusiastic, vigorous and whole-hearted. All subsequent aims for a good programme depend on achieving this first aim.

THE 'PHYSICAL' IN PHYSICAL EDUCATION

Aim 2 *Teach physical skills to develop neat, skilful, well-controlled, versatile movement*

We want pupils to enjoy moving well, safely and confidently in a variety of situations.

Physical Education makes a unique contribution to a child's physical development because:

- the activities are experienced at first hand. Children do not read or talk about them. They do, feel, experience, practise, develop and learn the activities and skills,

- the skills are as natural as most pupils' enthusiasm for moving. Pleasure and satisfaction are gained from moving, and there is the added bonus that the body remembers and can perform physical skills, learned earlier, well into post-school years,

- it caters for and appeals to the many interests and aptitudes of pupils, enabling them, eventually, to participate confidently in worthwhile physical and sociable activities.

The elements of a broad and balanced Physical Education programme are:

a vigorous, whole body action leading to normal, healthy growth – gymnastic activities, dance, games, athletic activities, swimming and outdoor activities;

b skilful body management – gymnastic activities, dance, games, athletic activities, swimming and outdoor activities;

c competitive activities – games, athletic activities, swimming;

d creative and aesthetic activities – dance and gymnastic activities;

e challenging experiences in a variety of outdoor environments – outdoor and adventurous activities, swimming.

A balanced Physical Education programme spanning the primary school years is one through which these five elements are experienced.

THE 'EDUCATION' IN PHYSICAL EDUCATION

Aim 3 *Help pupils to become good learners as well as good movers*

Knowledge, understanding and learning are achieved through a combination of doing, feeling and experiencing physical activity, and the mental process of thoughtful decision-making.

Pupils are challenged to think for themselves and plan ahead, making decisions about their actions. The teacher's 'Can you...?' or 'Show me...' challenges dictate the nature of the action, but the precise way of doing it is a thought process left to the pupil. 'Can you travel along the bench,' sets the action, while 'using hands and feet?' requires the pupil to decide on a personal response.

Refinement, adaptation, improvement and further thinking are inspired by the teacher's 'Can you include some travelling at different levels along your bench?' or 'Show me a direction change at one point in your travelling.'

Understanding is further developed by asking the class to watch a demonstration, think about and then comment on some aspect of what they have seen. They can be asked to reflect on what they thought was neat, pleasing, correct or inventive, and might be asked to suggest ways in which an action could be improved or developed.

Evaluation of self and of others then guides and informs the next stage of planning, extending the individual's knowledge and understanding, and contributing to an improved level of achievement.

It is helpful and fair to 'put the class in the picture' regarding the main aims and emphases of a new series of lessons. 'Our new lesson is about body parts and understanding how the different parts work and move.' Thereafter, whether rolling, upending, climbing, balancing, swinging or doing any of the many natural actions experienced during a typical Gymnastic Activities lesson, for example, the teacher will encourage the class to think about, feel, experience and learn to understand how their body parts work to support, receive and transfer their body weight.

Teachers and pupils should be focused, learning to do and learning to understand.

SELF-IMAGE AND FEELING VALUED

Aim 4 *Develop pupils' self-confidence and self-esteem by appreciating the importance of achievement, physically, to young pupils, by helping them to achieve, and by recognising, praising and sharing such achievements with others*

'An individual's regard for and attitude to his or her physical self, especially at primary school age, is important to the development of self-image and to the value given to self.'

Physical Education skills are natural, interesting and enjoyable for the majority of primary school pupils who participate enthusiastically. Skills can be learned and developed quickly, enabling pupils to experience success and enormous satisfaction.

Lessons are extremely visual and provide many opportunities for demonstrating improvement, success, creativity, versatility and enthusiastic performances. Such hard work and success should be recognised by the teacher, praised and commented on, and shared with others who should be encouraged to be warm in their praise and comments.

The teacher can see the whole class performing at all times. It is easy for him or her to give fairly continuous praise and encouragement to pupils of all ability levels if they are absorbed, working and practising hard to improve.

APPRECIATION OF OTHERS

Aim 5 *Develop desirable social qualities, helping pupils get on well with one another by bringing them together in mutual endeavours*

Friendly, co-operative, close relationships are an ever-present feature of Physical Education lessons. 'Our team; my partner; our group; our dance;' infer co-operative action, sharing of ideas or decision-making, and an awareness of, and consideration for, others' views.

With out-of-school play no longer a common feature of childhood, the many play-like, sociable experiences in Games, Dance and Gymnastic Activities lessons have become important contributors to social development.

Teachers need to recognise and value the many opportunities in lessons to: share space sensibly and safely with others; take turns at leading or following; demonstrate and be demonstrated to; combine with others to make a dance, invent a game or agree a sequence; or comment warmly and encouragingly about another's demonstration.

The height of consideration for others, of course, is to dress properly and quickly for lessons, behave well, disturbing neither teacher nor class, work quietly and safely without impeding others, and respond immediately to instructions.

THE PROGRAMME

Aim 6 *Satisfy every pupil's entitlement to achieve physical competence in a broad and balanced, Physical Education programme*

Ideally, a school's Physical Education programme provides weekly lessons in Games, Dance and Gymnastic Activities. In summer, infant classes can have a second Games lesson by reducing Dance and Gymnastic Activities to half a term each. Similarly, junior school Athletic Activities lessons are included in summer by reducing Dance and Gymnastic Activities to half a term each.

As well as satisfying pupils' entitlement to a satisfactory programme by allocating an adequate amount of time to these three main areas, we are providing at least the minimum of twenty minutes of physical activity, three times a week, recommended by the Royal College of Surgeons, to stimulate and exercise the heart for normal growth and development. 'This degree of activity,' the Royal College says, 'also seems to play an important role in improving an individual's sense of well-being.' Sufficient, vigorous exercise is good for your heart and makes you feel good. The Surgeons' report warns, 'There will need to be a change in society's attitude to exercise and remaining physically active.'

The College of Surgeons' concern for the nation's increasingly inactive lifestyle was echoed by the late 1980s Channel 4 programme *The Health Of Our Children*, where, it was reported, 96% of children are not doing the minimum amount of exercise required for normal heart development. Many children were 'sick at heart', many had coronary risk factors associated with middle age, and the situation was a 'medical timebomb' for the future. Professor Yacoub, a famous heart surgeon, emphasised the importance of exercise in childhood for the development of a normal, strong heart in adult life.

These concerns have had little effect on our schools or our nation. 'The Flab Generation' was the October 1997 headline in a national newspaper, describing British children as slothful and sedentary, with inactive lifestyles, just like their parents. 'A nation of flabby kids who are what they eat' refers to 'a rise in overweight children raised on a diet of high-fat, junk food and a dramatic reduction in physical activity.' A 2002 report revealed that one in ten British children under the age of four is obese, and up to a third of ten year olds do not even walk continuously for ten minutes a week. Experts now estimate that in a class of 30 children, 2 will have a heart attack, 3 will develop diabetes, and 13 will become obese, all as a result of a sedentary lifestyle and a diet dominated by chips, biscuits, crisps, sweets and sweet fizzy drinks.

Realistically, only in schools can we teach and encourage children to succeed in a wide range of physical skills to stimulate a desire for healthy activity throughout life. Equally, it is only in schools that the recommended level of regular physical activity for all children can be provided. Physical Education makes a unique contribution to an all-round education, but also makes a special contribution to the kind of lifestyle that might be pursued as adults.

CONTRIBUTIONS TO THE SCHOOL'S CURRICULAR AIMS

The Physical Education programme should identify how its particular aims fit in with the overall curriculum aims of the school. For example:

1 *'The school aims to provide a broad and balanced curriculum to offer a range of experiences which are relevant to the pupils' present and future needs.'*

Physical Education is central to the area of physical development within the whole curriculum. It makes a unique contribution to an all-round education by providing opportunities for every pupil to experience, feel, do and learn movement at first hand.

2 *'Our school aims to enable each pupil to experience success and achievement, and develop a positive self-image.'*

Physical Education activities are natural for young, growing pupils who participate enthusiastically. They can quickly experience success and a sense of achievement. Pupils' attitude to their physical selves is important to the development of their self-image.

3 *'Our school's curriculum aims to encourage positive interaction with others and within groups.'*

Participation in Physical Education is a continuously, highly social activity. Pupils are taught to show self-control, consideration and unselfishness when moving among others on a crowded floor, apparatus or playground. They work as members of groups and teams, co-operating in Games and Dance lessons particularly, to learn new skills which are then used to create their own dances and games. In Gymnastic Activities they co-operate to lift, carry, place, share and use apparatus safely. Participation in interested observation of others' performances and achievements is included in every lesson, as is the making of appreciative comments to encourage the performer and help the class generally.

4 *'Our school aims to create healthy minds and bodies.'*

A main feature of Physical Education teaching is its dual emphasis on performing and learning through:

a inspiring vigorous physical activity to promote normal, healthy growth and development as well as the ability to move well;

b promoting the learning processes of planning, adjusting and adapting. Judgements are made before, during and following activity. Results are assessed and subsequent actions are refined and improved.

TIMETABLING INDOOR LESSONS

'We can't fit them all in. There's not enough hall time,' is the excuse offered by schools when asked why they don't give every class a weekly lesson in Dance and Gymnastic Activities, in addition to the Games lesson which takes place out of doors.

Parents, particularly those keen for their children to experience a full and varied Physical Education programme, would not be pleased if a school claimed to be unable to find the twenty-eight sessions necessary to provide every class with two indoor lessons weekly, in a combined infant and junior school with two classes in each year. This is fewer than six indoor lessons daily.

A timetabling problem in some schools is caused by the excessive amount of 'dead time' before and after lunch. Many schools stop indoor lessons during the half hour before lunch, and start again half an hour after lunch. This often means that only one lesson is timetabled between morning break and lunch, and can mean the loss of one indoor lesson in the afternoon.

When school meals staff are asked to co-operate and delay coming into the hall until 11.45am, instead of 11.30am, to enable about two hundred more indoor lessons to be enjoyed every year, they are usually found to be willing – particularly if their own children are pupils of the school, and keen on their Physical Education lessons. Preparation of the hall for lunch, and clearing away afterwards, can be done in fifteen minutes.

If the pupils in classes timetabled to follow an assembly or a break can be changed into PE clothing beforehand, they will be able to make a prompt start and save up to ten minutes through not needing to change and travel all the way to and from their classrooms, en route to the hall.

A Headteacher once asked how long it should take a class to change for a Physical Education lesson. Some teachers claimed it took between ten and fifteen minutes. A class should take only three to five minutes to get ready. In the same way that pupils are aware of, and encouraged to improve and be proud of their times for running certain distances, they should be encouraged to improve and be proud of their times, as a class, for changing for their lessons. Some can get ready in less than two minutes. Each minute saved through quicker changing adds two hours per year to the lesson times. Quick changing by everyone means that every class can be in the hall, ready to start its lesson at the correct time. This leads to a full, satisfactory and enjoyable lesson with a prompt finish, allowing the next class to start on time.

SAFE PRACTICE AND ACCIDENT PREVENTION

In Physical Education lessons, where one of the main aims is to contribute to healthy growth and development, we must do everything possible to ensure safety and accident prevention.

Good supervision by the teacher at all times is a main contributor to safety. The first question asked after a serious injury is always, 'Was the teacher with the class?' He or she must be there and teaching from positions from which the majority of the class can be seen. This usually means circulating on the outside, looking in, with no-one behind his or her back.

Good teaching develops the correct, safe method of landing from a height; taking weight on the hands; gripping apparatus or rolling. The outward expression of the caring attitude we try to create is a sensible, unselfish sharing of hall floor, apparatus and playground, and self-control in avoiding others.

Badly behaved classes who do not respond immediately, starting or stopping as requested; who rush around selfishly and noisily, disturbing others; who are never quiet in their speech or their body movements; and who do not try to move well, are destructive of any prospect of high standards of safety or lesson enjoyment.

A safe environment requires a well-behaved, quiet, attentive and responsive class. Good behaviour must be continually pursued until it becomes the normal, expected way to work in every lesson.

The hall should be at a good working temperature, with windows and doors opened or closed as necessary, to cope with changing seasons and room temperatures. Potentially dangerous chairs, piano, tables or trolleys should be removed if possible, or pushed against a wall or into a corner. Floor sockets for securing bolts for ropes and climbing frames should be regularly cleared of cleaning substances which harden and block the small sockets.

On the playground, pupils should be taught to remain within the lines of the grids or netball courts to avoid running, dodging or chasing into fences, walls, sheds, seats or steps into buildings.

Before the lesson starts the teacher should check for sensible, safe clothing with no watches, rings or jewellery which can cause serious scarring and injury, as well as long trousers that can catch heels, and unbunched hair that can impede vision.

Indoors, barefoot work is recommended because it is quiet, provides a safe, strong grip on apparatus, and enhances the appearance of the work. Barefoot work also enables the little used muscles of the feet and ankles to develop as they grip, balance, support, propel and receive the body weight.

METHODS OF TEACHING PHYSICAL EDUCATION

During Physical Education the teacher is mostly involved in whole class teaching, with no help from the teaching aids that keep pupils busy and independently engaged in many of their classroom lessons. Even when talking to an individual, a pair or a group, the teacher still needs to be aware of the whole class. The inspiration for everything that happens comes from the teacher. He or she needs to be:

- well prepared to make the lesson full and enjoyable

- enthusiastic to create an equally enthusiastic response

- encouraging to help pupils feel successful and appreciated

- keen to inspire vigorous physical activity in pupils whose lifestyles are probably inactive and often sedentary.

The lesson plan is the teacher's essential guide and reminder of the current lesson's content. July's end of year lesson will only be at a sufficient stage of progression from the previous September's if all the lessons in between have been recorded. Failure to refer to a lesson plan results in the same or similar things being done month after month.

Staff unity regarding the type of lesson plan which pupils will be trained to follow is as important for whole school progression as it is regarding what we do and why we do it. Good lesson plans give teachers information and practical help and do more to inspire good Physical Education than anything else.

The 'scene of busy activity' ideal for every lesson needs an understanding by pupils that they should be 'found working, not waiting'. They need to be trained to respond quickly, behave well, keep on practising until told to stop, and avoid standing in queues.

The teacher needs to avoid using over-long explanations or too many demonstrations with lengthy comments by observers. Lessons that lose a lot of time end up with incomplete apparatus work, little time for playing games, and half-created dances with no time to share them with others.

Demonstrations and observations by pupils and teacher are essential teaching aids however, because we remember what we see – good quality work, safe, correct ways of performing, the exact meaning of terminology, and good examples of variety and contrasts.

Demonstrations can be organised as follows:

- all watch one, two or a small group

- half of class watch the other half and then change places

- each pupil watches a partner

- a pair watches a pair, then change places.

Shared choice or indirect teaching takes place when the teacher decides the nature of the activity, and challenges the class to decide the actions. Limits set are determined by the age and experience of the class. From the simple 'Can you travel on the apparatus, using hands and feet?' with its slight limitations, we can progress to 'Can you travel on the apparatus, using hands and feet, and include a balance, a direction change, and taking all your weight on your hands at some point?' Shared choice teaching produces a wide variety of results to add to the class (and the teacher's) repertoire. Being creative is extremely satisfying and most primary school pupils enjoy and are capable of making individual responses.

Direct teaching takes place when the teacher tells the class what to do, for example:

- any of the simple, traditional skills of gymnastics

- the correct way to throw, catch and do other games skills

- how to do a folk dance step or figure

- the correct, safe way to take body weight on hands

- the correct, safe way to grip apparatus to circle, climb or hang

- the correct, safe way to lift, carry and place apparatus.

If a class is restless, unresponsive, or doing poor work, a directed activity can restore interest and discipline, and provide ideas and a valuable starting point from which to develop.

Pupils who are less inventive or less gifted physically will benefit from direct teaching, particularly if the teacher suggests a simpler alternative. 'If you don't like rolling forwards, try to roll sideways. Start curled up on your back to keep your head out of the way.'

The stimulus of direct request is the kind of challenge many enjoy, and to which they respond enthusiastically. 'Can you and your partner bat your ball up and down between you, six times?'

National Curriculum implementation when teaching Physical Education can most easily and concisely be checked under the following three headings.

1 Is the class being challenged to make planned, thoughtful, safe responses?

2 Is neat, controlled, enthusiastic, almost non-stop performing, the most obvious feature of the lesson?

3 Are opportunities being provided for observing, reflecting on, and evaluating performances? Do pupils learn from such evaluation, planning, adapting and starting the whole process again?

FACILITIES AND EQUIPMENT

Teaching and developing Physical Education successfully requires appropriate facilities and sufficient equipment, with the following being recommended.

Gymnastic Activities

Juniors

Hall with climbing ropes and climbing frames
    12 × mats, 2 × 1m each

3 × 8ft 9in junior balance benches

1 × 3ft high, two-section barbox which can be divided into two smaller boxes with a padded platform on lower section

1 × 24in high and 1 × 30in high nesting table

1 pair each of lightweight 3ft, 4ft and 5ft high trestles

1 × 8ft metal pole and 3 × 8ft planks with two pairs of hooks as linking apparatus for trestles

Plus, for infants

2 × 18in high nesting tables

2 × 6ft infant balance benches

Games

Infants

Where no netball court is available, the playground 'classroom' is a painted rectangle of six or eight, 8–10 metre square grids.

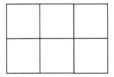   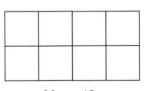

20m × 30m   *or*   20m × 40m

Sets of 30 of:
- small balls
- medium balls
- large balls
- bean bags
- skipping ropes
- wooden playbats
- hoops
- lightweight rackets and small foam balls for short tennis.

10 × rubber quoits

6 × 20cm foam balls

1 × set kwik cricket

10 × long, 24ft skipping ropes for group skipping and for making 'nets' for short tennis and quoits

Playground chalk

8 × marker cones

Inexpensive, zip-top, light plastic holdalls with handles for bulky equipment such as large balls and rackets, and small, plastic crates which can each hold 30 small balls, skipping ropes and bean bags as well as quoits and long ropes.

Plus, for juniors

1 or 2 netball courts

2 × sets netball apparatus

30 × hockey sticks

6 × playground hockey balls

6 × rugby balls

1 × set stoolball apparatus

SATISFACTORY STANDARDS

Physical Education lessons are so visual that most of the following headings for considering standards can be checked by an interested observer.

- **Vigorous physical activity** involves all pupils for most of the lesson.

- **Responsive pupils, behaving well**: obviously enjoying lessons; working hard to learn and improve skills; and exuding enthusiasm and concentration, are an uplifting feature of high standards.

- **Enthusiastic teaching, using praise and encouragement warmly**, stimulates pupils to even greater levels of endeavour. Praise is specific, referring to what is pleasing, to inform the pupil being praised, and to let others hear and learn. 'Well done, Susan. Your balances are still, firm and beautifully stretched.'

- **Skills, appropriate to the age group**, are taught and developed. There is an impression of neat, quiet, confident, well-controlled, successful performing with economy of effort. Pupils show understanding by remembering and repeating their movements.

- **Pupils' behaviour towards one another is excellent**. Undressing and dressing quickly to extend lesson time; safe, unselfish sharing of space and apparatus; working quietly to avoid lessons being stopped because of noise; observing demonstrations with interest and then making helpful, friendly comments; and co-operating well as partners and members of groups and teams, all indicate desirable standards of social behaviour.

- **Varied teaching styles** include:
  a indirect or shared choice teaching
  b direct teaching
  c good and varied use of demonstrations, observations, comments.

- **Satisfactory time allocation** provides regular, weekly lessons in Dance, Games and Gymnastic Activities – a broad programme which also includes Athletic Activities and Swimming for juniors.

- **Lesson plans** are in evidence as a reminder of all the parts of the current lesson and as a reminder of what has been taught so that the work can be progressed.

- **Sensibly dressed pupils** wear shorts, a T-shirt or blouse, and plimsolls. Indoors, barefoot work is recommended. As an example, the teacher should at least change into appropriate footwear.

- **Continuity and progression from year to year** are evident in the way that older pupils work harder for longer at increasingly difficult activities, demonstrating skill and versatility.

- **An awareness of safe practice and accident prevention** is evident in the way pupils share the limited space. The correct way to lift, carry and use apparatus, land, move, roll, support and use the body, generally, are regularly mentioned.

A PATTERN FOR TEACHING A SKILL OR PRACTICE

Excellent lesson 'pace' is expressed in almost non-stop activity with no bad behaviour stoppages and no 'dead spots' caused by long queues, over-long explanations or too many time-consuming demonstrations. The teaching of each of the skills which combine to make a lesson determines the quality of the lesson's pace – a main feature of an excellent Physical Education lesson.

A typical Games lesson, with its warm-up and footwork practices, skills practices and small-sided group practices and games, will include about a dozen skills. A Gymnastics Activities lesson will have about six floorwork actions and six to ten apparatus work skills. A Dance lesson includes warming-up activities, several movement-training skills, steps and patterns, and a dance climax.

Whatever the skill, there is a pattern for teaching it, as follows.

1 **Quickly into action**. In a few words, explain the task clearly and challenge the class to start. 'Can you stand, two big steps apart, and throw the small ball to your partner for a two-handed catch?' If a short demonstration is needed, the teacher can work with a pupil who has been alerted. Class practice should start quickly after the five seconds it took the teacher to make the challenge.

2 **Emphasise the main teaching points, one at a time, while the class is working**. A well-behaved class does not need to be stopped to listen to the next point. 'Hold both hands forwards to show your partner where to aim.' 'Watch the ball into your cupped hands.'

3 **Identify and praise good work while the class is working**. Comments are heard by all; remind the class of key points, and inspire the praised to even greater effort. 'Well done, Sarah and Daniel, you are throwing and catching at the right height and speed, and watching the ball right into your hands.'

4 **Teach for individual improvement while the class is working**. 'Patrick, hold both hands forward to give Christine a still target to aim at.' 'Ann and Alan, stand closer. You are too far apart.'

5 **A demonstration** can be used, briefly, to show good quality or an example of what is required. 'Stop, everyone, please, and watch how Cara and Michael let their hands "give" as they receive the ball, to stop it bouncing out again.' Less than twelve seconds later, all resume practising, understanding what 'giving hands' means.

6 **Very occasionally, to avoid taking too much activity time, a short demonstration can be followed by comments from pupils**. 'Stop and watch Leroy and Emily. Tell me what makes their throwing and catching so smooth and accurate.' The class watch about six throws and three or four comments are invited. For example, 'They are nicely balanced with one foot forward.' 'Their hands are well forward, to take the ball early, then "give" smoothly and gently.'

7 **Thanks are given to performers and those making helpful comments**. Further class practice takes place with reminders of the good things seen and commented on.

A PATTERN FOR LOOKING AT AND DEVELOPING 'MOVEMENT'

Knowledgeable observation of class activity by the teacher is the start of the whole development process. Comments and teaching points are based on what was seen. Looking for, and commenting on one thing at a time, is a good pattern to follow when progressing lessons to aid development.

1 **What actions are happening and how are the body parts working?** Teacher comments for improvement at Stage 1 are directed at the body parts concerned to stimulate neat, correct movements. 'Let your ankles stretch fully as you spring up, and give softly as you land.' 'Stretch arms forward or to sides to help your balance as you land from your jumps.'

2 **Body shape is always present.** At Stage 2 we want pupils to be aware of shapes and their contribution to the appearance and efficiency of movements. Poor, lazy, sagging shapes are unattractive and mean the body is not working hard. Firm, clear, strong, 'proud' shapes require physical effort and enhance performances. 'Really stretch your whole body from head to toes in your jumps.' 'Lift your head even higher as you stand, beautifully poised and stretched, ready to begin.'

3 **Where are the actions happening?** Is good, unselfish use being made of available space? At Stage 3 the emphasis is on enhancing the work by the interesting and contrasting use of own and whole room space, directions and levels. 'Travel along straight lines, following no-one.' 'Look for, then travel to the next open space.' 'Changing direction at some point would look very good.'

4 **Is good use being made of effort and speed to achieve neat, controlled performances, and to improve the quality, variety and contrast within performances?** Like body shape, effort and speed are ever-present features within actions. How firm or gentle? How explosive or soft? How fast or slow? By applying the right degree of force or speed at Stage 4, we make actions look more controlled, contrasting, interesting, and of better quality. 'Can you link slow, soft, "easy" jumps on the spot with a run into an explosive jump?' 'Contrast your lively, strong high jumps with your softer, gentler landings.'

5 **The climax of the development process is the eventual sequence of linked actions based on the planning, improvement and development that have taken place, ideally one step at a time, during the previous lessons.** In National Curriculum terms, the ability to 'show control in linking actions together' (KS1) and to 'repeat a series of movements performed previously with increasing control and accuracy' (KS2) are main requirements.

The quality of teacher observation will determine the quality of the eventual performance. Achievement of high standards will have been directly influenced by such observation.

Physical education in the National Curriculum

THE MAIN FEATURES

1 *A dual emphasis*: performing and learning

- **Planning**: pupils are challenged to plan their actions and responses thoughtfully.
- **Performing**: pupils are encouraged to work in a focused way, concentrating on the main features of the task.
- **Linking actions**: working harder for longer by planning and performing bigger, better, neater sequences.
- **Reflecting and evaluating**: pupils are helped to improve and progress as they adapt, change, develop and plan, guided by their own and others' judgements.

2 *Required activities*: Programmes of Study
Pupils should be taught:

	KS1	KS2
Games	**a** travel with, send and receive a ball and other equipment in different ways	**a** make up and play small-sided competitive games
	b develop these skills for simple net, striking/fielding and invasion-type games	**b** use skills and tactics and apply basic principles suitable for attacking and defending
	c play simple, competitive games that they and others have made	**c** work with others to keep the games going
Gymnastic Activities	**a** perform basic skills in travelling, stillness, finding and using space on floor and on apparatus	**a** create and perform fluent sequences on floor and on apparatus
	b choose and link skills and actions in short movement phrases	**b** include variations in level, speed and direction in their sequences
	c create and perform short, linked sequences with clear start, middle and end with contrast in direction, level and speed	
Dance	**a** use movement imaginatively, responding to varied stimuli, including music, and performing basic skills	**a** create and perform dances using a range of movement patterns, including those from different times, places and cultures
	b change the rhythm, speed, level and direction of their movements	**b** respond to a range of stimuli and accompaniment
	c create and perform dances using simple movement patterns, including those from different times and cultures	
	d express and communicate ideas and feelings	

3 *Attainment target*: Pupils should be able to demonstrate they can:

KS1

a select and use skills, actions and ideas appropriately, applying them with co-ordination and control

b vary, copy, repeat and link skills, actions and ideas in ways that suit the activities

c talk about differences between own and others' work; suggest improvements; and use this understanding to improve their own performance

d recognise and describe the changes that happen to the body during exercise

KS2

a link skills, techniques and ideas and apply them accurately showing precision, control and fluency

b compare and comment on skills, techniques and ideas used in own and others' work and use this understanding to improve their own performance by modifying and refining skills and techniques

c explain how the body reacts to different types of exercise and explain why regular, safe exercise is good for health and fitness

THE NATIONAL CURRICULUM'S MAIN QUESTIONS

1 Are pupils given opportunities to plan? 'Can you ...?' 'Can you show me ...?' 'Can you plan to ...?'

2 Is there an impression of pupils performing and improving?
Do they work hard to improve their neat, poised, confident actions and sequences?

3 Are pupils being challenged to build longer and better sequences by linking actions?
Are they working harder for longer with a clear beginning, middle and end to each sequence?

4 Are pupils given opportunities to reflect and make judgements on what they and others have done? Is practical use then made of this reflection to plan again to improve?

ASSESSMENT OF ACHIEVEMENT

It is a guiding principle and priority of the National Curriculum that all pupils will be helped to progress and achieve, and be told how they have progressed and what they have achieved.

We need to put pupils 'in the picture' regarding the intended outcome of lessons, to keep them focused on the essentials. 'This new lesson is about body shape. I want you to be able to show different shapes in stillness and while moving. Clear, firm body shapes make your work look neater and make you work harder.'

Pupils should also be told that assessment of their achievement is always of an overall performance, rather than the isolated parts that combine to make it – the whole gymnastic sequence, the taking part in a game, or the finished piece of dance, rather than an isolated skill within, will make more sense to the pupil.

This keeps all teachers focused on a proper climax to their lessons, with an adequate amount of time allocated to:

a apparatus work in Gymnastic Activities lessons, with clearly understood sequences

b games and practices within groups small enough for each pupil to be fully involved

c creating a dance, individually, in pairs, or in groups small enough for all to play an active part.

Because Physical Education is so visual, most judgements can be made by teacher observation, or during teacher and pupil observation when the class is watching something admirable. An added bonus is the potential that such observations have for helping observers and performers to improve.

Three headings summarise the areas within which we want our pupils to achieve. We want them to:

- perform successfully, demonstrating:
  a well-controlled, neat, accurate, safe work
  b the ability to perform and link skills together with control
  c wholehearted, enthusiastic and vigorous activity
  d a concern for own and others' safety, sharing space sensibly

- plan thoughtfully, thinking ahead to demonstrate:
  a good decision-making
  b sensible, safe judgements
  c good understanding of what was asked for
  d a willingness to listen and adapt to others' views

- evaluate and reflect on own and others' work to guide them as they adapt, develop and improve, demonstrating an ability to:
  a recognise and identify the most important features
  b express pleasure at the part of the performance enjoyed
  c suggest ways to bring about an improvement
  d self-evaluate and act upon own and others' reflections.

Games

'These features of games – play-like, challenging, vigorous, skilful and dependent on rules – give some indication of their appeal and potential as an educative medium.' (Movement, 1972)

Individual and team games are part of our national heritage and an essential part of the Physical Education programme.

Skills learned during Games lessons easily lend themselves to being practised away from school, alone or with friends or parents, and are the skills most likely to be used in participating in worthwhile physical and sociable activities long after leaving school – an important, long-term aim in Physical Education.

Vigorous, whole body activity in the fresh air promotes normal, healthy growth and physical development, stimulating the heart, lungs and big muscle groups, particularly the legs.

Games lessons come nearest of all Physical Education activities to demonstrating what we understand by the expression, 'Children at play'. Pupils are involved in play-like, exciting, adventurous chasing and dodging as they try to outwit opponents in games and competitive activities. Such close, friendly 'combat' with and against others can help to compensate for the increasingly isolated, over-protected, self-absorbed nature of much of today's childhood, with little healthy adventure.

Games lessons are taught outdoors, in the fresh air, in the playground. For infant classes, the playground 'classroom' can be a netball court, if the school has one, or a rectangle, subdivided into six or eight, 8–10 metre rectangles.

The junior school playground 'classroom' is one or two netball courts. A line in a different colour to the court and painted from the centre of the end line to the opposite end line, can be a centre line for games played across each third, and it can limit defenders or attackers to their own halves. The line can also be a 'net' for short tennis, quoits and volleyball.

The lesson starts with warming-up and footwork activities to improve stopping, starting, dodging, marking, running and jumping. Skills are taught individually, in pairs or in small groups in the middle part of the lesson. During the course of a year a wide variety of games equipment will be experienced, ideally with the same equipment being used by all in the same lesson, so that teaching applies to all. In the most important, final part of the lesson, three or four different practices or games provide an exciting and varied climax with near-continuous action for all.

Games will appeal to, and be very popular with, the majority of pupils if: the pupils are always moving; the games are exciting; nobody is left standing doing nothing; they are fun to play; there is plenty of action; and if rules prevent quarrels, let the game run smoothly, let all have a turn and prevent foul play.

GAMES IN THE PLAYGROUND

Infant Games lessons have always taken place in a playground, while most junior school Games lessons now take place on the playground rather than on an on-site or off-site playing field.

The advantages and attractions of playing games on the playground include:

- the lesson starts soon after leaving the class-room

- equipment does not need to be carried far
- the surface is suitable for all types of games
- the teacher can supervise and be heard easily
- shelter can be reached quickly if the weather deteriorates.

SAFETY ACTIVITY IN PLAYGROUND GAMES LESSONS

At the start of the school year, the teacher needs to make the class aware of the extent of their 'classroom' for Games lessons, namely the area contained within the four outside lines of the netball court or grid.

The teacher should explain to pupils why they are 'contained' for these lessons:

- the class can all be seen and they can all see the teacher
- the teacher can be heard by everyone without shouting
- demonstrations can be seen clearly by everyone
- comments made by pupils, following a demonstration, can be heard by all pupils
- surrounding, adjacent hazards such as fences, walls, sheds, seats, steps into buildings or

hutted classrooms, and climbing equipment, all need to be avoided by fast moving, dodging and chasing pupils, to avoid serious accidents.

Other safety considerations include:

- wearing safe clothing and footwear with no watches, jewellery, long trousers that catch heels, or unbunched, long hair that impedes vision
- good behaviour with instant responses to instructions, and quiet voices and feet, enabling all to hear
- good supervision and circulation by the watchful teacher, mainly from the outside looking in, able to see everyone
- good teaching, particularly of the footwork skills of stopping, starting, dodging and changing direction.

THE THREE GROUPS WITHIN GAMES

GROUP 1 INVASION OR RUNNING GAMES

Skills: Throw, catch; kick, head; strike, collect; carry, propel.

Games such as football, netball, hockey, basketball and rugby are our most popular games and can be played all year round. They are the only type suitable in winter because of their lively running.

Invasion games are difficult, needing a high level of physical, intellectual and social skill to outwit close marking opponents and combine

with team-mates to advance the ball. Simplified versions must be used to keep the numbers per team down to one or two, and up to five at the most. A small playing area is essential to simplify the advancing of the ball. Scoring must also be fairly simple to achieve, such as arriving on a line, holding the ball.

GROUP 2 NET GAMES

Skills: Throw, strike, bat, aim, return; as in short tennis, tennis, quoits, volleyball and badminton.

A simple 'net' can be one of the painted lines of the playing rectangle, a chalk line, an 8-metre skipping rope tied between netball posts or chairs, or a light net tied between posts.

Net games are the simplest of the three types of games and the one group in which you are not restricted to using a ball. Quoits, bean bags, shuttlecocks, as well as balls, can be struck, thrown, aimed and returned over the line or net. The court is small, with the opposing players on separate sides. With little distraction, long rallies of continuous play can be enjoyed.

The rather static nature of net games with little vigorous running, particularly for young learners, makes them more suitable for warmer weather, from late spring until autumn.

GROUP 3 STRIKING/FIELDING GAMES

Skills: Strike, bat, bowl, field, catch, collect, aim, throw.

In games such as cricket, rounders and stool ball, the one or two batting players receive and strike the ball to score, competing against all the other players of the fielding side.

A high level of hand and eye co-ordination is needed to contact well with the ball. For inexpert, younger pupils with poor batting skills, the game can become stagnant, boring and with too little action to keep the fielding side interested and involved.

These games are more suitable for warm weather and should be played in small groups of two, three, four or five at the most. 'Tip and run' or 'Non-stop cricket' are used to stimulate action, as players continuously change roles of bowler, batter, backstop and fielder. Simple rules aim to keep the action moving. 'When you hit the ball, you must run round the skittle and back.' This gives fielders the opportunity to be active, running the batter out.

THROWING AND CATCHING PRACTICES

Throwing and catching are the two most frequently used skills in primary school Games lessons. They are widely used in the small-sided versions of invasion games such as netball, basketball and rugby; in net games such as volleyball and all its simplified versions, down to young infants throwing a bean bag over a line or rope 'net'; and in striking/fielding games such as cricket, rounders and stoolball, they are used continuously.

THROWING AND CATCHING PRACTICES AND GAMES FOR INFANTS

Individual practices

1 One hand to other hand.

2 One hand to both hands.

3 Two hands to two hands.

4 Throw up, clap, catch.

5 Little throw, catch; medium throw, catch; higher throw, catch.

6 Throw up and forward a little way, run to catch.

7 Aim bean bag at nearby line or mark. Pick up, aim at new mark.

8 Walk, let the ball bounce, catch with both hands.

9 Jog, throw and catch just in front of eyes with cupped hands.

10 Jog, throw and catch. On 'Change!', put ball down and find another.

Partner practices

1 Walk side by side, handing bean bag to partner's two hands.

2 Throw and catch, two metres apart, two hands to two hands.

3 One hand to throw, two to catch. Partner's hands well forward.

4 Catch low, below knees; medium at waist; higher at head height.

5 Aim the ball at a line between the two partners. Partner catches after bounce. Count hits on the line.

6 Throw. Move apart. Throw. One or two more moves, then back again.

7 Walk side by side, throwing just ahead of partner's hands.

8 Follow the leader who shows ways to throw and catch.

9 One throws straight to partner who bounces it back.

10 Throw to partner. Move to a new space for return throw.

Group practices and small-sided games

1 Aiming contest in twos to land bean bag in hoop, 2–3 metres away.

2 Aiming contest through high hoop held by partner. Best of three.

3 Walk, throwing and catching bean bag. From two metres, aim to land it in one of the hoops. (Several scattered in the area.)

4 One partner stands still, the other jogs around for throw and catch.

5 Follow leader, throwing and catching, trying one and two-handed ways to practise. Change and see if follower can remember them.

6 Bean bag each on a line, three metres apart. Aim at partner's line. Change places, pick up own bag and repeat.

7 Partners at long rope 'net'. How many throws over net without dropping bean bag? Throw with one hand to two hands reaching.

8 Bean bag among three. 'Piggy in the middle', with pairs trying to throw to each other, keeping it away from one in middle.

9 'Wandering ball' with three of the group outside the circle, passing ball across to bypass and outwit one in the circle.

10 Team passing, three against one, with the three keeping close enough to receive catches but give the one a chance to intercept.

11 Two versus two, or four versus four, end line touch with several agreed ways to score. For example, touch ball down on end line; bounce it in one of the hoops in corners; pass to partner on end line.

THROWING AND CATCHING PRACTICES AND GAMES FOR JUNIORS

Individual practices

1 Throw above head a short distance, jump to catch at full stretch and land, balanced.

2 Show at least three ways to throw and catch (e.g. one hand to same; one to two; at different heights; on the move and still).

3 How many sets of low, medium and high catches can you make before missing a catch, on the move, jogging around?

4 Stand with ball held, ready. When the teacher calls 'Forward; backward; to left; to right!', throw the ball up a short distance in that direction, then run to catch it.

Partners or small group practices

1 Run, side by side, passing ball ahead of partner, rugby style.

2 'Fake' to pass a chest pass to partner. Bounce pass it and move to a new space.

3 Teams of three, passing. Pass to team-mate who moves to a new space.

4 All pairs in one third of whole court area, making short 2–3-metre passes, at different heights and speeds, to avoid the many others also practising in the same third.

5 Two against one, with the two interpassing to touch dodger with the ball.

6 Run, passing to partner. On 'Change!' ball is put down on ground and each player finds a new partner and a different ball.

7 Aiming practice at a line, starting one metre back, and moving back a step at a time to find the limit of accurate throwing.

Small-sided games and group practices

1 Two versus one, where one is passive, keeping between the two, but not trying to intercept. Change the 'one' often.

2 Two versus one, fully competitive, where three passes equals a goal.

3 Invent a game in threes to develop throwing, catching and running into spaces, e.g. two versus one, where one marks partner without the ball to make this player dodge free to receive the ball.

4 Ball among four, in half of third of court. Two versus two, with attackers having '3 lives', trying to score on opponents' line.

5 Rugby touch, four against four, scoring by passing to team-mate catcher on opponents' line, or by touching ball down on end line.

6 Invent a game with emphasis on throwing and catching, e.g. three versus one rounders. Fielders make three catches before batter runs round diamond, to get batter 'out'.

7 Four versus four, heading ball. Score by heading large foam ball over opponents' line, after receiving pass from team-mate.

8 Four- or five-a-side skittleball, mini-basketball, netball or handball. What is the main rule? How do we re-start after a score? How can we encourage more scoring? (e.g. defenders will be passive while attackers are in their own half to let attackers advance the ball easily to at least half way).

THE INFANTS SCHOOL GAMES LESSON

Warm-up and Footwork Practices provide a lively start, put the class in the mood for activity, and aim to improve the quality of the running, jumping, chasing, dodging, marking and changing speed and direction.

Skills Practices form the middle part of the lesson, ideally with all using the same implement so that teaching can apply to everyone. Almost without exception, infant lessons will include:

- individual practices which allow maximum opportunity to improve as pupils practise with ball, bean bag, skipping rope, hoop, quoit, bat or racket and ball

- partner practices to experience the unpredictable behaviour of a ball, for example coming at different heights, speeds and angles as it does in a game. In co-operative partner practices, partners help each other to master the skills. In competitive partner practices the challenging nature of games, with their testing of skills and wits, and their striving to overcome an adversary, are experienced.

Small Group Practices and Games are the climax of the lesson, receiving fifteen minutes to allow five minutes for each of the three different activities. This most important part of the lesson must be given its full time allocation, even if it means cutting other parts short. One of the three activities will always use the implement and the skills practised in the middle of the lesson.

ORGANISATION OF THE GROUP PRACTICES AND GAMES PART OF THE LESSON

At the start of the year the class is divided into three mixed groups. They are trained to go and stand in their own starting rectangle within the grids or thirds of the netball court area, when asked to 'Please go to your starting places for group activities.' The three sets of implements to be used will have been placed adjacent to, but outside, the enclosed rectangle where they will be used. Balls, bean bags and skipping ropes, for example, are contained within plastic crates to keep them tidily together.

The teacher checks that the numbers in each third are correct. If one third has absentees, some pupils are transferred from another group. Then the teacher says, for example, 'Please collect your rope, ball between two, or bean bag between two for your first activity.' When all are standing ready, implement in hand, or beside a partner, the teacher gives a brief explanation of each activity before saying 'Please begin'.

During the three following lessons of this stage of development, group activities start with the instruction 'Please go to your starting group places', easily remembered from the previous lesson. They are asked to collect their first activity implement before being told to begin. The teacher circulates round the three different practices or games, reminding them of the main teaching points, progressing the work, giving praise and occasionally presenting a demonstration.

Reception Winter 30 minutes

Emphasis on: **(a)** vigorous, immediate responses to become and stay winter-warm; **(b)** good footwork – dodging, chasing and changing direction; **(c)** enjoying learning to control a big ball.

WARM-UP AND FOOTWORK PRACTICES – 5 minutes

1 Show me some lively ways you can travel to visit all parts of our playground 'classroom'. Travel quietly, please.

2 Mostly we go forwards, but some movements can be done going sideways. Can you show me some (e.g. slipping, skipping, bouncing)?

3 'Free and Caught', with a quarter of the class wearing bands as chasers. If caught, stand still with hands on head. Those not caught can free you by touching your elbow. Changing direction suddenly is a good way to dodge. (Chasers should be changed often.)

SKILLS PRACTICES; WITH A LARGE BALL – 10 minutes

Individual practices

1 Walk or jog using two hands to throw the ball just above your head. Catch it with two hands just in front of your eyes, thumbs behind and fingers well spread.

2 Keep walking and bounce the ball down just in front of you with both hands pushing. Catch the ball as it bounces back up.

3 Practise freely with your ball to show me how you can send it and then collect it. Remember to keep inside the lines of our 'classroom' (e.g. kick, throw, bounce, head, roll).

Partner practices

1 Stand facing your partner, about two big steps apart. Can one of you send the ball straight to your partner and the other one send it back with a little bounce between you (i.e. chest and bounce passes)? Use both hands each time, aiming carefully.

2 Like rugby players, can you jog side by side, and either throw a gentle, easy pass or hand it carefully to your partner?

3 Have some free practice, sending the ball to your partner in a favourite way that seems to work for the two of you.

GROUP PRACTICES AND GAMES – 15 minutes

Follow the leader, with a choice of quoits, bean bags, hoops or balls

'Follow' means going somewhere, moving to keep warm. Leader, do something simple.

Large ball with a partner

Can you invent a simple game? e.g. throw for header; aim at line contest; kick to each other; chase to touch ball.

Free practice with a skipping rope in one or both hands, or on the ground

Try skipping with a slow pull of rope along ground, or run and jump over rope.

Year 1 Summer 30 minutes

Emphasis on: **(a)** demonstrating increasing control over body and implements; **(b)** demonstrating the ability and desire to practise to improve.

WARM-UP AND FOOTWORK PRACTICES – 5 minutes

1 Follow your leader who will demonstrate a lively sequence of a short walk, a short run and a jump. Watch your partner's feet carefully and see if the two of you can build up to moving in the same way, together. (Variety of small or large movements, bent or stretched legs, one or both feet take-offs, landings.)

2 Six cross-court sprints. Partners stand side by side down middle of court. On the signal 'Go!', both race back to touch one side line with one foot and race back to touch partner's hand. (After six times teacher calls out 'First... second... third...')

SKILLS PRACTICES; WITH A SMALL BAT AND BALL – 10 minutes

Individual practices

1 Can you bat the ball upwards softly to about head height, using your wrist rather than your elbow or shoulder as the moving part?

2 Can you repeat this, walking forward, and try to catch the ball, balanced still, on the bat, every so often? From this balance, start hitting it up again.

3 Can you bat the ball upwards from being held ready in the non-batting hand, let it bounce once, bat it up, then catch it, and start again?

Partner practices

1 Batter, strike the ball gently for partner (two metres away) to catch with both hands. After six catches, change duties.

2 Can you stand side by side, both batting upwards gently? When you have agreed your best team score, change to both batting down, counting your best score.

GROUP PRACTICES AND GAMES – 15 minutes

Skipping rope each

Can your group show ways to use a rope, including skipping, alone or with a partner.

One small bat and ball among three

Can you invent a simple game that uses bowling and batting in a small space? e.g. Two versus one batter who must run when ball is hit. Fielders get batter 'out' in agreed ways.

Partners – one quoit

Rope 'net' tied between chairs. One versus one quoits, trying to score by landing quoit on opponent's side for a point.

Throw with one and catch with two hands.

Year 2 | Autumn | 30 minutes

Emphasis on: **(a)** practising, almost non-stop to improve; **(b)** practising good footwork, including dodging and chasing; **(c)** practising varied ball skills.

WARM-UP AND FOOTWORK PRACTICES – 5 minutes

1 Run, practising little side steps to avoid others coming towards you. In a side step one foot goes out to the side instead of forward to put you on to a new line, still facing the same way.

2 5-points tag. All have 5 points to start with. When touched you lose one of your points. (NB No dangerous pushing, touch gently.)

SKILLS PRACTICES; WITH A LARGE OR MEDIUM BALL – 10 minutes

Individual practices

1 Walk, throwing the ball just above your head and catching. Keep your fingers spread, thumbs back, fingers round the sides.

2 Bounce the ball using your fingertips, left and right hands, on the spot, and weaving in and out of the others.

3 Dribble the ball like a footballer, keeping it close. When I call 'Stop!' see how quickly you can control the ball by placing a foot on top of it to make it still.

Partner practices

1 Stand about three metres apart, throw a two-handed pass to your partner and move sideways into a space for the return pass, still only three metres apart. Pass; move; receive.

2 Shadow dribbling, one ball. Leader shows partner favourite ways to dribble, using feet or hands. After six variations, change over and see if the follower can copy the routine exactly.

GROUP PRACTICES AND GAMES – 15 minutes

Quoits with a partner, 1 v 1

Long rope 'net' tied between chairs. Play quoits and try to score by landing quoit on opponent's side for a point.

Decide how to start, how many points to a game, and any other rules to help the game.

Large ball among four, 3 v 1

'Wandering ball' with three of group on outside of big chalk circle passing ball across circle, to pass and outwit the one in the circle.

Keep changing one in centre who works hard to intercept the ball.

Partners with a hoop each

Stand at opposite sides of court from partner. Bowl hoop to pass each other and go to partner's line.

Keep close to, and in control of, hoop.

Now can you show me another good partner practice?

THE JUNIOR SCHOOL GAMES LESSON

Warm-up and Footwork Practices aim to get the class quickly into action, stimulate vigorous, leg muscle activity which, in turn, stimulates the heart and lungs.

Pupils enjoy practising running, jumping, chasing, dodging, marking, changing speed and direction, side-stepping, swerving and accelerating. Older juniors learn correct stopping and starting so that footwork rules in netball and basketball are understood. 'Faking' by moving head, shoulder or foot to one side, then moving the opposite way; sprint and change of direction dodges; and offensive and defensive footwork, used in 'one on one' dodges, are all practised.

Skills Practices form the middle part of the lesson with the whole class using the same implement and practising the same skills so that all teaching and coaching applies to everyone

With younger, less experienced pupils the practices include individual then partner practices of skills they might have performed before. They progress on to co-operative and competitive, partner and small group, practices of skills already experienced to make practising more like the game situation.

Group Practices and Small-sided Games can provide one of the most eagerly anticipated parts of all junior school Physical Education. They are the climax of the lesson and must be started promptly to allow their full time allocation. One of the three games or activities always includes use of the implement and skills practised in the middle part of the lesson. The three games take place in the thirds of a netball court. If a second court is available, it can be used for any activity that benefits from a bigger playing pitch.

The main organisational problem is explaining and starting this final part of the lesson on the first day of a new series of lessons. At the start of the year, the six teams or groups will have been chosen and given a 'Starting place for games and group activities'. If the teacher explains only one game at a time, to the ten about to play it, the remaining twenty will be standing waiting, losing heat and patience, and often becoming noisy and inattentive.

The answer is to have all three groups playing the same game, one of the three new ones to be introduced. Instructions about scoring, the main rules and method of re-starting after a score, will apply to all. The signal 'Start!' applies to everyone.

When all three games are being played sensibly, the teacher moves to and teaches one group its proper, planned game or activity. When this group is going well, the teacher goes to and teaches a second group its planned activity. The teacher then says 'Stop, everyone, and look at each of the two new games some of you have not seen yet.' Each new game is demonstrated with an accompanying commentary from the teacher. The three groups then rotate on to their second activity, and finally to their third and last activity.

Year 3 | Winter | 30–45 minutes

WARM-UP AND FOOTWORK PRACTICES – 4–6 minutes

1 Jogging is an easy, quiet form of running, with arms hanging low and heels not as high as in normal running. Practise easy jogging at a speed you think you can easily keep going for two minutes.

2 10-points tag, all against all. All have 10 points to start with. Each time someone touches you, you lose a point. (NB Gentle touching, no pushing. Check who has the most points left and who caught the most, after each 12–15 second game.)

SKILLS PRACTICES; WITH HOCKEY STICKS AND BALLS – 8–12 minutes

Individual practices

1 Run, carrying the stick with the right hand straight down at side, as if carrying a suitcase. The right hand should be in the middle of the stick, flat side to the left, and head of stick pointing forward.

2 When I call 'Change!' place left hand at the top of stick, leaving right hand where it is. Carry in front, the head of the stick near the ground as if about to receive a ball. Keep running. (Change between (1) and (2) several times.)

3 With your ball now, keep the flat side of the stick forward and slightly to the right. Push the ball gently in front of you, along a straight line.

Partner practices

1 Your partner is three metres away. Dribble round your partner and back to your starting place. Push the ball to partner who repeats the practice.

2 Walk side by side, gently sending the ball in front of each other.

GROUP PRACTICES AND SMALL-SIDED GAMES – 18–27 minutes

Hockey stick and ball each

Walk with ball 'glued' to stick. When you see a space about 2–3 metres ahead, push pass ball into the space. Run after ball and repeat.

Emphasise low stick in front of you at all times. No high follow-through.

Large ball among four, 2 v 2, half pitch

Attackers try to score, rugby style, by touch down over opponents' line; by a pass to partner on line; or into one or more hoops which can be additional scoring systems.

When touched by defender, you must pass the ball.

Large ball between two

Allowing one bounce on the ground in between hits, keep your best score when juggling the ball to keep it up and bouncing, using foot, thigh or head.

A sort of 'football tennis' on the spot.

Year 4 | Summer | 30–45 minutes

WARM-UP AND FOOTWORK PRACTICES – 4–6 minutes

1 Stay in one third of the netball court, space out sensibly and find out how many (a) long hops, (b) bounding steps and (c) jumps from two feet to two feet, you need to take to cross your third from line to line.

2 Now run round the whole netball court, jogging one third, sprinting the middle third, jogging the end third. Turn back and repeat.

SKILLS PRACTICES; WITH SHORT TENNIS RACKETS AND BALLS – 8–12 minutes

Individual practices

1 Walk, bouncing the ball up on the face of the racket.

2 Walk, hitting the ball up, letting it bounce and hitting it up. Use soft hits.

Partner practices

1 One throws gently underarm to partner's forehand. Partner with the racket does forehand hit back for catch by bowling partner.

2 Have little rallies with each other, emphasising 'side on' position when hitting.

GROUP PRACTICES AND SMALL-SIDED GAMES – 18–27 minutes

Hoop each

Can you make up a sequence that includes three ways to use your hoop? (e.g. throw up and catch; walk bowling; skip on the spot in hoop.)

Short tennis in twos

Throw over rope 'net' (long rope tied between netball posts) for forehand return by partner. A hoop on bowler's side can be target for return strike.

Tunnel ball rounders, four- or five-a-side

All batting team follow striker to score a point for each of four cones reached before fielding team passes ball through tunnel of legs to end person.

Year 5 | Winter | 30–45 minutes

WARM-UP AND FOOTWORK PRACTICES – 4–6 minutes

1 In your running, practise side steps and direction changes to avoid others coming towards you.

2 One against one, across court, line to line, dodging and marking, with dodger trying to get past the marker using good footwork and fakes. Change duties back to starting line.

SKILLS PRACTICES; WITH LARGE BALLS – 11–15 minutes

Partner practices

1 Standing about three metres apart, make a two-handed pass from beside shoulder aimed above partner's head for a jump and catch. Pass to running partner. Run to a new space to jump to catch.

2 Juggle ball with foot, thigh or head to keep it bouncing once, under control between you and your partner.

3 One versus one, screening the ball, while dribbling with foot to protect the ball from pursuing partner.

4 Invent a one versus one game using throwing, juggling or screening already practised (e.g. 'football tennis' over a line 'net').

GROUP PRACTICES AND SMALL-SIDED GAMES – 15–24 minutes

Team passing, four- or five-a-side, one large ball	Free netball, four- or five-a-side	Floor football, four- or five-a-side, slightly flat ball
Pass to team-mate in a space and not too far from you, ideally three metres.	Players are free to move anywhere on court and all are allowed to shoot.	Score by arriving on opponents' goal line with ball under foot. Keep ball below knee height which is easier with a flattish ball.
Grab ball into stomach on receipt.	No dribbling. Pass and move forward, ready for return.	Defenders stay in own half. Attackers stay in opponents' half to create more open game with lots of spaces.
Four good passes equals a goal.	One point for near miss, hitting hoop. Two points for a goal, through hoop.	
Vary passes to include chest, bounce and overhead passes.	If overcrowding round ball is spoiling play, ask teams for solution (e.g. one defender stays in own half).	To encourage open passing and unselfish play, agree that two passes may be made before a tackle is made by an opponent.

Year 6 — Summer — 30–45 minutes

WARM-UP AND FOOTWORK PRACTICES – 4–5 minutes

1 Run anti-clockwise around netball court, then jog over the end third, sprint over the middle third, and jog over the end third. Turn and repeat. Count how many strides you take to cross the middle third. Try to reduce this by better knee lift and stronger rear leg action.

2 In twos, side line sprint relay. Stand side by side down centre of court. On the signal, race to touch nearer side line, then touch partner who races to touch his or her side line. Make ten side line touches. Go!

SKILL PRACTICES; WITH SHORT TENNIS RACKETS AND BALLS – 6–10 minutes

Partner practices

1 Standing about four metres apart, one bowls underhand to batting partner who strikes the ball back, using forehand to bowler. Change over after eight hits, Which couple can make most catches before dropping one?

2 Have a competition with your partner, alternating striking ball up a short distance using forehand and backhand grips, i.e. palm facing up, then knuckles facing up.

GROUP PRACTICES AND SMALL-SIDED GAMES – 20–30 minutes

2 v 2, short tennis

Drop on end line, serve with a forehand hit. Change sides after 4-point games.

```
X  |  O

X  |  O
```

Tip and run cricket, four- or five-a-side

Batting team X
Fielding team O

```
              O
              III
              X

      O             O

   X          X
   X          III
              O
```

Volleyball, four-a-side over high rope net between netball posts

Allow three volleys on each side of net. Score while serving. Team rotates after a loss of service.

```
      X3 ——→ X4

      X2 ←—— X1
```

1 Challenge short tennis teams to suggest appropriate, fair ways to serve to start and restart the games, e.g. a drop and hit from behind own line to person diagonally opposite.

2 Challenge tip and run cricketers to agree a way to keep the game moving so that no out-standing batters keep one team at wicket, e.g. batters help to field before and after being 'in'.

3 Challenge volleyers to agree one 'friendly' rule to help keep game movingt, e.g. one bounce is allowed on each side.

PROGRESSING A GAMES LESSON OVER 4 OR 5 LESSONS

Gymnastic Activities and Dance lessons can begin at a simple level of performing the actions neatly, because they are natural and easy. The challenge for the teacher and class is then to plan and develop movement sequences that link these natural actions together, and refine them by adding 'movement elements' such as changes of shape, direction, speed and tension.

Developing a Games lesson is different from the above because the eventual target is the mastery of the specific games skills included in the lesson. Such skills include:

- good footwork used in stopping, starting, changing direction, chasing after and dodging away from other players

- sending, receiving and travelling with a ball in invasion, striking/fielding and net games, and controlling other games implements such as skipping ropes, quoits, hoops and bean bags

- inventing games with agreed rules in co-operation with a partner or small group. Fairness, safety, lots of action and an understanding of the need for rules are the intended outcomes

- playing competitive games as individuals, with partners, and in small-sided teams

- understanding the skills and particular roles of players as they attack and defend in the three types of games.

Often the starting point, practising the new skill, is a problem, because controlling the implement is difficult. Balls, bats, hoops, skipping ropes, rackets, quoits and bean bags behave unpredictably and the teacher has to simplify the planned skills to enable pupils to succeed and progress in subsequent lessons. Reception class pupils, for example, might have to walk beside a partner, handing the bean bag or ball to each other, before progressing to throwing and catching.

The varied skills headings listed above fit neatly into both infant and junior Games lessons with their:

- footwork skills practices

- skills practices, which can include 'invent a game'

- practices and small-sided games, which can include 'invent a game' and challenges to suggest ways to improve a game with a new rule, other ways to score, or limits on player movement.

Step by step, revising the previous lesson's work, and introducing only one new teaching point at a time, the teacher progresses the skills of the lesson.

Year 1   Winter   30 minutes

LESSON 1 OF A 4-LESSON DEVELOPMENT

Emphasis on: travelling with, sending and receiving a ball.

WARM-UP AND FOOTWORK PRACTICES – 5 minutes

1 Can you run quietly, looking for spaces to run through?

2 Keep running, but change direction when I call 'Change!'. Push hard with one foot to make you go the other way.

3 Play dodge with a partner. You may only catch your partner when he or she is not 'safe' on a line (i.e. on a line is untouchable, but encourage regular excursions and change chasing and dodging duties often).

SKILLS PRACTICES; WITH A LARGE BALL – 10 minutes

Individual practices

1 Throw the ball up with both hands, then catch, walking. Aim to throw up to head height and just in front of you for an easy catch, just in front of eyes.

2 Throw the ball up and a little in front of you and let it bounce on the ground. Run after it and catch with both hands after the bounce.

3 Show me another way to send the ball a little distance, then collect it and send it again (e.g. kick, head, roll, bounce).

Partner practices

1 Stand two metres apart. Thrower, throw slightly to one side of your partner who has to move quickly to collect the ball.

2 Use both hands to bounce the ball just in front of your partner for a catch. Bounce it about one metre in front of him or her.

3 Can you invent a standing practice for sending the ball to a partner? Then try to invent a moving practice for sending it.

GROUP PRACTICES AND GAMES – 15 minutes

Skipping rope each to practise freely	Partners sending large ball to each other	Hoops 'tag' with three chasers and seven dodgers
Practise freely, but try skipping on the spot and on the move.	Can you send the ball a short distance to each other, on the spot and moving?	Dodgers are 'safe' when sheltering in a hoop. If caught, dodgers become chasers.
Can you run over the rope, one foot after the other? Which is your leading leg?	A 'short distance' means 2–3 metres only. Stay close.	Can you do a change of direction to dodge away?
On the spot, can you do a double beat of your feet on each turn of the rope?	Variety can include throwing, heading, kicking, bouncing.	Chasers, remember to touch gently and safely.

Year 1 — Winter — 30 minutes

LESSON 2 OF A 4-LESSON DEVELOPMENT

WARM-UP AND FOOTWORK PRACTICES – 5 minutes

1 Can you run on tiptoes, lifting heels and knees, to make your running quiet?

2 Change direction suddenly when I call 'Change!' Press down hard with one foot to make you go the other way. Practise going to left and to right. Change!

3 Be good sports and keep leaving the line in your dodging game with a partner. Try direction changes to get away, rather than fast and sometimes dangerous running.

SKILLS PRACTICES; WITH A LARGE BALL – 10 minutes

Individual practices

1 As you walk, throw the ball up and forward with both hands, to just above head height. Show me your eyes looking at the ball.

2 Throw it up and forward a little higher so it bounces up for you to run and catch with both hands. Use a nice long arm swing into your throw and run quickly to be in the right place to catch.

3 Now show me another way to send the ball, then collect it. Look for good spaces and don't disturb others. I see throws, kicks, bounces, headers, rolls. Well done.

Partner practices

1 Throw to one side for your partner to run to catch. Catcher, move early to arrive and be standing, still, ready for the catch.

2 In bounce passing, bend the arms until the ball touches the chest, then stretch arms firmly for a long push into the bounce. Spread fingers at the sides of the ball to catch it.

3 Show me your invented ways of throwing and catching, one standing and one on the move. Keep close for lots of practice.

GROUP PRACTICES AND GAMES – 15 minutes

Skipping rope each to practise freely	Partners sending large ball to each other	Hoops 'tag' with three chasers and seven dodgers
Try slow running over the rope. Use a small, turning wrist action with hands out wide at waist height. On the spot, try a jump and bounce: 1, 2; 1, 2; for each turn of the rope.	Show me slow jogging, side by side, sending the ball to each other. You can hand, throw, bounce or kick. Now send it from a standing position, then run to a new space for the return throw, kick, bounce, roll or header.	When caught, take a coloured band and be a chaser. Dodgers, can you show me good changes of speed or direction to get away? See which you like better. Chasers, touch gently please.

Year 1   Winter   30 minutes

LESSON 3 OF A 4-LESSON DEVELOPMENT

WARM-UP AND FOOTWORK PRACTICES – 5 minutes

1 Run to visit every part of our playground 'classroom' – ends, sides, as well as the middle. Let me see you looking for spaces.

2 Let's all stay in this middle area. Jog round and do quick little direction changes to avoid some-one coming towards you. Is there one side you like going to better than the other?

3 In our line dodging game, listen for my 'Change!' which means you all change what you are doing – dodgers become chasers, and chasers become dodgers. Keep listening ... change!

SKILLS PRACTICES; WITH A LARGE BALL – 10 minutes

Individual practices

1 Can you jog, slowly, throwing the ball up and forward for a catch at head height? Spread fingers round the sides of the ball for the throws and catches. Use a nice smooth throwing action.

2 Throw the ball up and forward into a good space and let it bounce up to about chest height for an easy, two-handed catch. Try to 'feel' how strongly you need to throw it for a good bounce.

3 What is your best score in keeping the ball bouncing up and down? Try with one hand, two hands, a foot, a head, always with a bounce in between touches with the different body parts.

Partner practices

1 Throw the ball into a space to one side of your partner to make your partner run to catch it. Catcher, can you be so quick at moving that you are standing still, ready for an easy catch?

2 Make a bounce throw to land just in front of your partner's feet. Catch the ball with straight arms, then bend them fully before sending the next throw to your partner.

3 Can you invent a lively, nearly non-stop, way to practise sending the ball to each other? You will need to be close together and probably using both hands (e.g. one bounce, then one straight).

GROUP PRACTICES AND GAMES – 15 minutes

Skipping rope each to practise freely	Partners sending large ball to each other	Hoops 'tag' with three chasers and seven dodgers
Skip to travel from space to space. Then show me skipping in that space.	Standing still, practise throwing at three heights, low by knees, middle by chest, and high at head height.	Today, let's do quick walking only, to dodge and chase.
Feet and hand actions should look 'easy', with quiet running or bouncing, and wrists turning the rope.	Make partner move to receive the ball now. Move to a new space after sending the ball.	Dodgers, use quick direction changes.

Chasers, spread out. Try to trap them in a corner. |

Year 1   Winter   30 minutes

LESSON 4 OF A 4-LESSON DEVELOPMENT

WARM-UP AND FOOTWORK PRACTICES – 5 minutes

1 Run quicker when you have lots of space. Run slower, or even on the spot, when it is suddenly very crowded.

2 Keep running, but practise your sudden direction changes when you come to a line, or meet someone coming towards you.

3 For our safe line dodging game, can you think of a rule to keep the game moving? 'Dodgers must move after chasing partner counts slowly to three,' is a good suggestion. Let's all try it.

SKILLS PRACTICES; WITH A LARGE BALL – 10 minutes

Individual practices

1 As you walk or jog, throwing the ball up and forward for a two-handed catch, always be looking for good spaces to move into. Throw, catch, look for space; throw, catch, look for space.

2 Throwing higher and further to make the ball bounce for a chest height catch means it is important to look for a big space to throw and run into. Use a long, smooth, arm push throw.

3 Show me your favourite way to send the ball without it running or bouncing far away from you. Send, collect; send, collect, and make it look easy. Good ideas might be worth copying.

Partner practices

1 Receiving partner, signal with your arm to show which way you want to run to receive the throw from your partner. Point, then run to receive the ball and catch it, standing ready and still.

2 Stand still to receive the ball bounced to land in front of your feet. After bouncing it, move to a new space, ready for the next bounce. Throw, move to space, catch; throw, move to space, catch.

3 Both you and your partner choose how to send the ball to each other. Each of you might plan a way. Maybe one will have a standing way and the other a moving way. Stay close for lots of action.

GROUP PRACTICES AND GAMES – 15 minutes

Skipping rope each to practise freely, skipping on the spot and moving	Partners sending large ball to each other	Hoops 'tag' with three chasers and seven dodgers
On the spot, try the slow double beat and the quicker single beat. Then show me neat, non-stop, skipping travelling. Pretend your group is on a stage, all doing your best skipping.	Walk side by side throwing like rugby players, swinging arms across your body to throw just in front of partner. Change from throwing to show me another way you like sending the ball.	Dodgers, use quick walking or easy jogging as you do your changes of direction to get away. My 'Change!' means everyone changes duties. Change!

Year 5   Winter   30–45 minutes

LESSON 1 OF A 4- OR 5-LESSON DEVELOPMENT

Emphasis on: sending, receiving and travelling with a ball, and playing simplified versions of recognised competitive games.

WARM-UP AND FOOTWORK PRACTICES – 4–6 minutes

1 Run, emphasising good 'straight ahead' position of head, arms, shoulders and legs. Visit all parts of our playground classroom.

2 Dodge and mark with partner. Marker chases dodger. On my 'Stop!', see who is the winner: the dodger who can't be touched by partner, or the marker who can touch dodger. (Change places and repeat.)

SKILLS PRACTICES; WITH RUGBY OR LARGE BALLS – 8–12 minutes

Individual practices

1 Run, carrying the ball in front of you and letting it swing from side to side naturally, using both hands. Hands, with fingers spread, hold the sides of the ball; arms are straight.

2 Throw the ball above the head a short distance. Jump to catch it at full stretch and grab it in to your chest with both hands. Don't jump too early. Wait until the ball starts to come down.

Partner practices

1 Jog side by side, passing the ball just in front of your partner for an easy, two-handed catch. Change sides often to let you practise passing to both left and right sides. A slightly high pass to the chest is better than a low one down by the knees.

SMALL-SIDED GAMES; IN THIRDS OF NETBALL COURT – 18–27 minutes

Rugby touch four- or five-a-side

Score by placing the ball on the ground with two hands, behind opponents' line.

Re-start after score at centre by pass back by team scored against.

Tackle by two hands touching opponent's hips.

Run straight and fast until tackled, then look for a running team-mate to pass to.

Ground football, four- or five-a-side

Score by arriving on opponents' line, with the ball under control, under foot.

Re-start after score by kick in from the end line by team scored against.

Use a flattish ball to keep the ball below knee height.

Pass often, dribble seldom. The passed ball is quicker than one dribbled.

Hockey, four- or five-a-side

Score through a 3-metre wide goal by push made in opponents' half.

Ball must be pushed by the stick, starting on ground, behind the ball. No hitting with long back-swing or high, dangerous follow-through.

Advance ball quickly by aiming it ahead of a running team-mate.

Year 5 — Winter — 30–45 minutes

LESSON 2 OF A 4- OR 5-LESSON DEVELOPMENT

WARM-UP AND FOOTWORK PRACTICES – 4–6 minutes

1 In your best 'straight ahead' running, can you feel your head, shoulders, arms and feet pointing and going straight ahead?

2 Reaching your leading knee up and forward, and using your rear foot to push you hard forward, also help good straight running.

3 Dodge and mark in twos. On my 'Stop!', stop immediately so that the real winner is seen. If either of you takes a step after my call the wrong person appears to be the winner.

4 Use dodges to get away from your partner rather than fast sprints. Dodging and trying to keep up with a dodger are important games skills. Try a sudden change of direction or speed to lose your partner.

SKILLS PRACTICES; WITH RUGBY OR LARGE BALLS – 8–12 minutes

Individual practices

1 As you run, carrying the ball low in front of you as in rugby, can you let your arms swing naturally from side to side and pretend to pass to each side?

2 Keep your feet pointing straight ahead, as we practised earlier, and twist your whole upper body to turn towards the person you are pretending to pass to.

3 Jog easily forward and when you have space, throw the ball above head height a short distance. Run and jump up to catch it at full stretch and grab it in to your chest with both hands.

Partner practices

1 Jog side by side, feet pointing straight ahead, and pass the ball just in front of your partner, for an easy, two-handed catch.

2 Keep arms straight as in rugby, as they swing from the shoulders. Do not bend and stretch in your elbows. Pass to the right when the right leg is forward, and to the left when the left leg is forward.

SMALL-SIDED GAMES; IN THIRDS OF NETBALL COURT – 18–27 minutes

Rugby touch, four- or five-aside	Ground football, four- or five-a-side	Hockey, four- or five-a-side
Pass immediately you are tackled, preferably to a team-mate running to receive a short pass as we practised.	Keep ball below the knee by controlling it before passing it.	Carry stick low in front of you to stop high, dangerous stick movements.
Try 'dummy' passes to make opponents go the other way.	Defenders, stay back to make more space for your forwards to dribble, pass or shoot.	No tackling in the opponents' half to help the game flow.
	Pass, then follow, to be ready for the next pass.	Move into a space as a signal for a pass.

Year 5 | Winter | 30–45 minutes

LESSON 3 OF A 4- OR 5-LESSON DEVELOPMENT

WARM-UP AND FOOTWORK PRACTICES – 4–6 minutes

1 In your best 'straight ahead' running, visit every part of the netball court. Feel your hands, shoulders and feet keeping square to the front. There should be no side to side twisting.

2 If you have to slow down or run on the spot when you are in a crowd, still continue your best straight ahead running.

3 In dodge and mark, dodge away from your partner with changes of direction or speed. Try one of each to find out which is the more unexpected and the more successful for you.

4 When I call 'Stop!', stop at once or the wrong person will be the winner. A winning dodge means your partner cannot reach and touch you.

SKILLS PRACTICES; WITH RUGBY OR LARGE BALLS – 8–12 minutes

Individual practices

1 Run, carrying the ball low in front of you like a rugby player. Let both arms swing naturally from side to side and practise 'dummy' passes to each side with a full turn of your upper body, looking to where you would be passing.

2 Keep your feet pointing straight ahead as we practised earlier; no sideways, crab-like running which cannot be done at speed.

3 Jog, and when you see a space ahead, throw the ball just above head height. Run and jump to catch it with both hands at full stretch. Grab it in to your chest.

Partner practices

1 Jog side by side, feet pointing straight ahead, and pass the ball, just in front of your partner, for an easy, two-handed catch. Change sides often or run the other way to practise passing left and right.

2 Remember – straight arms as in rugby, swinging from the shoulders, rather than from the elbows, across the leg on the side being passed to.

SMALL-SIDED GAMES; IN THIRDS OF NETBALL COURT – 18–27 minutes

Rugby touch, four- or five-a-side

Avoid long back passes where the ball ends up a long way behind where it was.

A short scissors pass to a team-mate running across and behind you is often an unexpected move.

Sprint straight until tackled.

Ground football, four- or five-a-side

Forwards will stay in opponents' half to make more space in both halves.

Let's try '3-touch' football – receive; push forward, looking; pass to moving teammate. Stationary team-mates make space by keeping out of the way.

Hockey, four- or five-a-side

The ball travels fastest in this one of the three games. Pass please!

If you pass to a stationary player you are expected to run on for the return pass.

If someone runs on, you should pass ahead of them.

Year 5 Winter 30–45 minutes

LESSON 4 AND 5 OF A 4- OR 5-LESSON DEVELOPMENT

WARM-UP AND FOOTWORK PRACTICES – 4–6 minutes

1 As you run along straight lines to all parts of the court, focus on reaching straight ahead with all moving body parts. An occasional side-step to avoid someone will bring you back on to the same straight line, one step width to the left or right side.

2 In dodge and mark, try head, shoulder and foot 'fakes' or short sprints to one side to make your partner go that way, then suddenly going the opposite way, to be unmarked.

SKILLS PRACTICES; WITH RUGBY OR LARGE BALLS – 8–12 minutes

Individual practices

1 Run, carrying the ball in front of you, and let it swing from side to side towards each forward foot. If someone runs towards you, pretend he or she is an opponent and throw a 'fake' pass, looking that way to make it seem real.

2 Continue running, and when you see a space ahead, throw the ball up above head height and time your leap to catch the ball at full stretch with both hands. Grab the ball in to the chest for security.

Partner practices

1 Invent a practice to develop running, passing and catching, as in rugby (e.g. player A runs on straight line; player B passes to A and runs close behind him or her to receive a short scissors pass; B passes back to A and runs behind A, to receive a second scissors pass. Make four passes and change over).

SMALL-SIDED GAMES; IN THIRDS OF NETBALL COURT – 18–27 minutes

Rugby touch, four- or five-a-side	Ground football, four- or five-a-side	Hockey, four- or five-a-side

All stand in team positions. Hands up the two forwards... the two defenders... the centres. Now, point at the opponent you will mark when their team has the ball. When you defend, keep in line between your opponent and your goal and make it hard for them to pass, receive a pass, or travel with the ball. Please begin.

Let running with the ball be your main method of attack, always with someone near to pass or 'dummy' to.	Centre, be a 'target' player, with your back to the opponents' line, to receive a pass for a shot or to pass back to team-mate.	Defenders, advance the ball quickly in one or two passes, then stay in own half to make room for own attack.

Stop! Have you any suggestions for improving your game by a new rule or an extra way of scoring (e.g. in rugby, allow forward passes in own half. In football, allow attackers one pass unimpeded in own half. In hockey, do not tackle in opponents' half)?

TEACHING HOW TO DEFEND IN INVASION GAMES

Most of the following practices, up to Stage 5, can be used with infants. Stage 5, two against two practices, would be included in the 'Group Practices and Games' final part of an infant school Games lesson.

Defensive footwork practices without a ball

Stage 1 – *individual practice* of starting, stopping, side-stepping, changing direction, running backwards and sideways.

Running sideways or backwards to mark an opponent for example, is most unnatural and has to be learned slowly. In the 'boxer's shuffle' with its rapid pattering of feet, the feet are apart, hips are low and the weight is forward. The feet never come together or cross over as the defender impedes the attacker's movements.

Stage 2 – *co-operative practices with a partner* provide easy but unpredicted changes of footwork. When following, you have to recognise and respond as though in a game. When leading, you have to understand the many footwork skills you can use in different situations – avoiding others, going for a space, changing speed and direction, feinting to deceive and outwit.

1 Follow your leader, who will change speed and direction.

2 Run beside a partner, keeping together. Leader does short sprint dodges for partner to respond to.

3 Run, one behind the other, at the same speed. The following partner sprints to just ahead of the leading partner, to become new leader.

Stage 3 – *competitive practices with a partner* give practice in responding to the sudden, unexpected movements of an opponent, without the ball, that will occur during games. We learn to use dodges and feints to break free from a close marking opponent.

1 Dodge and mark. Dodger tries to keep out of reach of marker.

2 One against one. Defender 'shuffles' backwards and sideways, trying to impede dodger's progress across court.

3 Partners face each other at the centre of the court. Dodger sprints to one side and stops suddenly, hoping defender reacts late.

4 Partners face each other. Dodger feints to one side with head, foot or shoulder to make defender start to move that way. Dodger then sprints the other way.

Competitive, defensive footwork practices with a ball

Stage 4 – *one against one practices* against a partner who is travelling with a ball, as in games such as football or hockey. Attacker dribbles to score. Defender has back to own goal line and tries to keep 'in line' between attacker and target line to force attacker to slow down, change direction or advance with difficulty.

In '3 lives' games the attacker starts the game three times from centre of area. After attacks break down three times because the ball was stolen or went out of area, the two players change roles. These can be practised in 'Skills Practices' section of lesson, or can be one of the three 'Group Practices and Small-Sided Games'.

Stage 5 – *two against two, defensive footwork practices with a ball, can be of two kinds:*

a '3 lives', one way games, in small area of the court. Attackers with the ball start five metres from the target line and score by arriving on the line with the ball under control. Each defender stays with an opponent to make passing or receiving, travelling with the ball, or progressing difficult. Couples change over after three starts by one pair. Both defenders use rapid, lively foot movements and try to take a space before opponents have time to go there;

b both teams try to score in end to end games. In early stages, if defenders defend passively, keeping in line but not trying to 'steal' possession, the attacking team advances the ball more easily, leading to more scoring opportunities.

Progress to **half court marking**, in which the attacking team is allowed to advance the ball to the half way line unimpeded. As attackers cross the half way line, the defenders mark them, trying to upset their forward progress, passing, catching and movement.

Full court marking, the next stage, is the most vigorous and lively form, making continuous demands on the team without the ball. Defenders pursue the player they are marking all over the playing area, using good footwork to impede the attackers. Full court, 'one on one' defence is an excellent way to become and stay warm in winter, but is difficult at first. In the early stages, the teacher can call 'Freeze!' With everyone perfectly still, he or she can see how well the defenders are staying in the correct position for marking, that is, in line between opponent and target line goal. Too often, defenders chase after the player with the ball.

Stage 6 – *playing three-, four- or five-a-side games* across one third of the netball court if only one court is available, or across two thirds for two of the games if two courts are available for the three small-sided games section of the lesson.

These lively running games will include simplified versions of recognised competitive games – netball, football, basketball, hockey, rugby and handball. In addition, there will be games that the teacher and class have invented for variety, such as headingball, skittle ball, or hoop ball with scoring by heading over a line, striking a skittle or by bouncing the ball in a hoop.

Successful 'one on one' team defending skills will be as well praised by the teacher as good attacking and scoring skills. The teacher will explain that 'Attacking is more difficult than defending, because you have the ball and yourselves to manage. There will be days when you don't attack well. However, your defending can always be good if you run, chase and make life difficult for your opponent. It's good being in a team who enjoy defending vigorously. If the opponents do not score, you will at least make a draw.'

TEACHING HOW TO ATTACK IN INVASION GAMES

Offensive footwork practices without a ball

Stage 1 – *individual practices* of actions that develop control, good balance, quick reactions and confident, 'poised' movement in the many situations experienced while moving among a class in the confined space of one netball court or set of grids.

Starting, stopping, changing direction, side-stepping, accelerating, sprinting, pivoting, balancing, dodging and feinting with head, foot or shoulder are all offensive footwork skills that need to be practised without the distraction of an opponent.

1 Run, looking for spaces, suddenly to sprint through.

2 Run freely and change direction on 'Change!'

3 Mix walking, jogging and sprinting where the space is available.

4 Practise side-steps on to a new line, still facing the same way.

5 Run. When I call 'Stop!', show me a balance on the nearest line.

6 Jog when near others, sprint when you have lots of room.

Stage 2 – *co-operative practices with a partner* who reacts to the several, unexpected offensive footwork skills to let offender see how successful they are. Reacting partner might say 'Good dodge!'; 'Good direction change!'; 'Brilliant side-step!' or 'Very good head fake had me going the wrong way.' The teacher emphasises that 'The attackers, with or without the ball, use dodges, body feints, changes of direction and speed to be free for just a moment so that they can make or receive a pass, find a space, or go for goal.'

1 Follow your leader, who will try some simple dodges to lose you. Following partner, help with friendly comments when deserved.

2 Follow your leader, who will change speed and direction suddenly to surprise you. Which is more successful for you?

3 Jog side by side, at the same speed. Leader does a sudden sprint to be free for a moment. Follower catches up and you repeat it.

4 Partners face each other, one metre apart. 'Attacking' partner progresses forward with small, rapid steps to try to make marker lose the 'in line' position, between attacker and target line.

Stage 3 – *competitive practices with a partner* give the 'attacking' player of the couple practice in checking the success of his or her repertoire of offensive dodges.

1 'Tag', where dodger tries to avoid being touched by chaser who then becomes the dodger. Teacher emphasises: 'Use dodges to avoid being caught, not high speed sprinting away.'

2 Dodge and mark. Marker tries to stay within touching distance of dodger on teacher's 'Stop!'

3 One against one, across court. Attacker uses feints of head, foot and shoulder, and direction and speed changes in order to evade defender.

4 Facing each other at the centre of the court, dodger tries a sprint dodge with a dash to one side, a sudden stop, then a sprint on to the same line or back to the opposite line before marker can respond.

Offensive footwork practices, using a ball

Stage 4 – *one against one practices with a partner* who marks you and impedes your progress as you try to reach the goal line with the ball still in your possession in dribbling games such as football, hockey or basketball. These little games need only a stretch of line as 'goal' and a five-metre approach to the line. Pairs decide the main rules. Teacher can allocate a number of minutes for each to attack, or they can play '3 lives' games with the same attacker starting three times, then changing roles.

Stage 5 – *two against two, practices with a ball* can be of two kinds:

a '3 lives', with the same pair of attackers starting three times from about a five-metre approach. After your three turns as attackers are used up,

attackers become defenders. '3 lives' games are good because players are all concentrating on, and trying hard to do one thing at a time;

b end to end games across a third of the court, with both teams trying to score. Passive defending, with the defending pair marking and keeping in line between the attackers and goal line, but not tackling, encourages a flowing, enjoyable game for the less experienced.

Half court marking lets the attacker bring the ball, unimpeded, to the half way line. Defenders then challenge strongly, trying to intercept the ball or make passing, catching and progressing difficult.

Full court marking gives the attacking pair a big problem as defenders chase them all over the court. Attackers need to use all offensive footwork, body feints, and passing and catching skills.

Stage 6 – *playing three-, four- or five-a-side games*, including scaled-down netball, hockey, basketball, football, handball, new image rugby and teacher and pupil created games such as headingball, skittleball and hoop ball. For optimum benefit, it is essential that the defenders keep to their 'one on one' marking of their own opponent, rather than all chasing after the attacking player with the ball.

Attacking players should ideally understand what is being tried:

a pass, then move to a new position. Receiver of pass knows that one player, at least, is trying to be available. Give and go!;

b a named team-mate moves quickly to the opponents' goal line when his or her own team has possession. This 'target player' receives a pass to score or return to a running, supporting team-mate;

c a 'Fast break' every time your team suddenly steals possession. During that change of possession, none of your team is marked. Do not hold on to the ball. Pass it quickly to an advancing team-mate;

d play wide in attack to pull your opponents away from the middle and leave more room for passes to an advancing team-mate;

e stay out of the play sometimes, keeping your opponent with you, to leave more room for someone better placed. Five-a-side is very crowded if everyone is moving and going for the pass.

Examples of successful team offensives, with pupils working well together to a simple plan, deserve to be demonstrated, praised and copied.

Reception | Games programme

AUTUMN

1 Respond quickly to instructions, particularly to 'Stop!'
2 Listen to teacher while practising. Try to respond to teaching points being made.
3 Share playground safely with others, looking for quiet spaces in all areas of playing area.
4 Stop on signal and change to next instruction. 'On "Stop!" show me a still balance on tiptoes. Stop!'
5 Travel in a variety of ways – walk, run, jump, hop, bounce, skip, gallop.
6 Practise diligently by yourself to learn and remember skills.
7 Experiment with one-handed throws and two-handed catches with bean bags, standing and on the move.
8 Practise throw and catch with medium ball, standing and moving.
9 Aim quoit at line or mark, with swing back and forward of arm.
10 Co-operate wtih partner, throwing and catching bean bag, quoit and medium ball, about 1 metre apart.
11 Practise freely with hoop on ground – jumps, balances; and in one or both hands – skipping, bowling.
12 Practise simple chasing and dodging games very carefully.
13 Participate wholeheartedly in these outdoor lessons.
14 Show actions to help others.
15 Watch demonstrations with interest. Say what was pleasing.

SPRING

1 Respond immediately and safely to instructions. Work hard to improve and remember skills.
2 Continue practising, almost without stopping, until asked to change to a new activity.
3 Run quietly with good lift of knees, heels, arms, upper body.
4 Respond enthusiastically to challenges to try things out and experiment.
5 Practise vigorously to keep warm in winter.
6 Practise to improve travelling actions such as run, jump, hop, skip, hopscotch, bounce.
7 Throw bean bag, ball, quoit to different heights and catch – low, medium, high.
8 Throw a big ball up, let it bounce, catch with both hands.
9 Dodge with good footwork, changing direction and speed.
10 Co-operate with partner in simple throw and catch, 1 metre apart, and while walking side by side.
11 Send medium ball to partner in a variety of ways – throw, kick, head, bounce, roll.
12 Link simple actions – throw and catch; run and jump.
13 Show better control over bean bag, ball, quoit, hoop and rope,
14 Observe others and point out features admired.

SUMMER

1 Respond readily, quietly, safely to instructions.
2 Show positive attitude to taking part. 'These lessons are fun, good for you, and exciting.'
3 Control body in motion; practise to gain confidence.
4 Experiment with varied implements – ball, hoop, quoit, small playbat.
5 Use feet well at take-off and landing from long and high jumps.
6 Extend variety and quality by listening well to instructions.
7 Use left and right hands to throw small ball up, then catch with two hands, standing and on the move.
8 Throw ball up and forward, run and catch with both hands.
9 Be versatile with hoop, bat and ball, ball, bean bag and quoit.
10 Remain in own third of court during group activities and practices.
11 Dodge and mark with enthusiasm and controlled use of space.
12 Follow a leader, using a range of implements, copying actions.
13 Make short rally with partner, throwing quoit or bean bag over line or long rope 'net'.
14 Throw ball or bean bag to partner using good judgement of height and force needed for success.
15 Link simple actions – walk, run, jump.
16 Comment on demonstrations and why they are neat, quiet and correct.

Year 1

Games programme

AUTUMN	SPRING	SUMMER
1 Respond readily and safely to instructions.	**1** Show improved body management in many skills, and display increasing self-confidence.	**1** Practise running for quality and variety with speed and direction changes, always conscious of good sharing of space.
2 Contribute to class tradition of quiet, almost non-stop work, listening to the teacher.	**2** Keep practising to improve and remember simple skills.	**2** Run and jump long and high to experience different actions, take-offs and landings.
3 Run and jump with vigour, good spacing, and lifting of heels, knees, arms and chest.	**3** Use varied implements in a variety of ways – ball, rope, hoop, quoit, bean bag, bat.	**3** Enjoy safe, enthusiastic chasing and dodging games.
4 Practise with wide range of implements – rope, ball, hoop, bean bag, quoit, playbat.	**4** Be keen on dodging and chasing games, using good footwork, with speed and direction changes.	**4** Show more confidence in using games implements – bat and ball, bean bag, rope, quoit, hoop, ball.
5 Practise many ways to send and control a ball – throw, strike, kick, head, gather, carry.	**5** Practise skills with a partner with increasing control and understanding, trying to please.	**5** Be physically active with good attitude to exercise in fresh air. 'It's good for you, makes you fit and it's good fun.'
6 Experience pleasure and excitement through achievement.	**6** Perform linked movements – run and jump; throw, run, catch.	**6** Show increased control in sending, receiving and travelling with a ball alone, and with a partner.
7 Practise with a rope to jump over, balance along, and learn to skip.	**7** Respond well to praise and encouragement.	**7** Practise bat and ball skills carefully, adapting to learn from experience, alone and with a partner.
8 Plan to respond to challenge – 'Can you … ?'	**8** Learn to skip in a variety of ways to keep warm in winter.	**8** Skip in many ways, on the spot and travelling in many directions.
9 Aim bean bag at hoop on ground or held high by partner.	**9** Invent a simple game with a partner, to use, for example, a ball, a line and a hoop. Agree the main rule and how to score.	**9** Show improved hand and eye co-ordination with a partner, throwing quoit or bean bag over a net.
10 Perform vigorously to become and stay warm in cold weather.	**10** Play a simple 2 v 2 game in a small area. Decide main rules and how to score and re-start.	**10** Link movements smoothly. Skip on spot and moving; bat down for 3, bat up for 3.
11 Co-operate with partner in leading and following, and in showing favourite activities.	**11** Watch less skilful 'learners' demonstrating and encourage them.	**11** Describe what was done and how it was done. Identify the quality admired.
12 Send a big ball to partner for an easy catch, trying out a variety of ways.	**12** Be able and willing to use good points seen and discussed during demonstrations.	**12** Make up and play simple games with a partner and 2 v 2, agreeing scoring system, main rules and how to re-start.
13 Demonstrate with enthusiasm.		
14 Observe demonstrations. Point out features that are worth copying.		

Year 2 — Games programme

AUTUMN	SPRING	SUMMER
1 Respond readily and vigorously to instructions.	1 Respond immediately and safely, showing a whole-hearted attitude in the pursuit of improved skill.	1 Show improved ability in running, hurdling, and jumping high and long.
2 Practise, almost non-stop, to improve.	2 Plan and practise thoughtfully, almost without stopping – repeating, adapting, improving.	2 Show good control in sending and receiving a ball, alone and with a partner – bat, bowl, throw, roll, serve.
3 Show good space awareness, avoiding others, for continuous, safe, undisturbed practice.	3 Link movements together with increasing versatility and control, using games equipment with skill, confidence and enthusiasm.	3 Continue practising with a wide range of implements – racket and ball, rope, hoop, bean bag, quoit.
4 Run and jump strongly, with good, relaxed arm, leg and upper body carriage, tall and poised.	4 Demonstrate knowledge and understanding as well as skill in well-planned performances.	4 Practise hand and racket short tennis over line or net co-operatively with a partner, and, when ready, competitively, agreeing how to serve, score and keep the game going.
5 Play chasing and dodging games with good footwork, and changes of speed and direction.	5 Show increasing awareness of ways to receive, send and travel with a ball.	5 Invent a game in 2s or 4s, in a small area, deciding scoring systems, the main rules, and how to re-start after scoring.
6 Plan to practise a variety of skills with ball, bat, bean bag, hoop, rope, quoit, racket.	6 Make up and play simple games with little equipment and few, simple rules.	6 Practise to improve skipping of all kinds, including follow a leader and group skipping with a long rope.
7 Link movements with increasing control, keeping action going to work harder for longer.	7 Work vigorously to keep warm.	7 Play 1 v 1, 2 v 2, 3 v 1, 3 v 3, and 4 v 4 competitive games, depending on skill levels of batting, bowling, fielding; serving, striking, returning.
8 Co-operate with a partner to: send, receive and travel with a ball; rally over net with ball and quoit, lead and follow.	8 Chase and dodge, changing speed and direction, to avoid being caught.	8 Link series of simple actions – skip on spot and moving; throw, run, catch; run to field, pick up, throw in; throw to self, bat up, catch, jump high and long.
9 Pass a big ball to partner, then move to a new space for the return pass. Give and go!	9 Co-operate with a partner to improve skills with ball, bean bag, bat, rope.	9 Display fair play, honest competition and good sporting behaviour.
10 Play 3 v 1, with the '3' keeping ball from '1' by passing and moving to space for next pass.	10 Play simple 1 v 1, 2 v 1, 3 v 1 and 2 v 2 games in a limited space, with simple rules and scoring systems.	10 With partners and in groups, invent and play simple versions of well known games like tennis and cricket.
11 Make up and play simple games with e.g. one ball, two hoops and a limited area. Decide the main rules, how to score and re-start.	11 Demonstrate skills willingly, and be keen to learn from and use helpful constructive comments made.	11 Describe what you and others are doing, and make simple judgements on a performance.
12 Pick out the main features in a demonstration and praise them.		

Year 3 — Games programme

AUTUMN	SPRING	SUMMER
1 Respond quickly to instructions and follow relevant rules.	1 Continue to develop skill and versatility in sending, receiving and travelling with a ball.	1 Practise to develop the skills of striking/fielding and net games, individually, in pairs, and in small groups and teams.
2 Share space sensibly for own and others' safety.	2 Practise skills individually, with a partner and in small practices and games.	2 Perform confidently, with the ability to make quick decisions.
3 Understand dangers of unsuitable clothing, footwear and jewellery.	3 Show safety awareness in games activities, particularly in sharing limited space in fast moving games and practices.	3 Play and create small-sided versions of recognised net and striking/fielding games, sharing decisions on scoring systems, the main rules and how to re-start.
4 Improve skills learned previously, in sending, receiving and travelling with a ball.	4 Develop neat footwork with quick reactions to avoid others and to evade close-marking opponents.	4 Discuss good sporting attitudes and recognise the need for rules regarding size of areas and effective boundaries.
5 Improve passing, then running into a space to receive a pass.	5 Plan, make up and play own games with set limits and agreed rules and scoring systems.	5 Understand common skills and principles in net and striking/fielding games, e.g. 'good length' ball in tennis or cricket; moving early to be still and ready to catch in cricket or hit in tennis.
6 Practise to improve in a well-planned, thoughtful way.	6 Learn, habitually, to move to a new space after passing a ball, often 'faking' to pass or run the opposite way.	6 Understand differing roles and duties as members of teams and groups in net and striking/fielding games. (E.g. bat, bowl, field, keep wickets.)
7 Understand the use of side-steps, direction and speed changes to evade a close-marking opponent.	7 Understand and improve '1 on 1' marking to keep 'in line' between an opponent and his/her target line.	7 Enjoy playing co-operatively to develop skill, and playing competitively to test skill.
8 Apply skills in simple games.	8 Respond safely, alone, and with others, to challenging tasks, often to 'Keep going, non-stop, to improve and to keep warm'.	8 Observe demonstrations with interest and suggest ways to improve a performance.
9 Co-operate with a partner to develop skills in co-operative and competitive situations.	9 Experience small-sided (1 v 1 up to 4 v 4) games, often of the half court, '3 lives' variety.	
10 Move vigorously to maintain warmth in colder weather.	10 Make simple judgements on own and others' performance.	
11 Improve dodging and marking skills in games situations.		
12 Show adaptability by quick responses to the unexpected.		
13 Observe others working and answer questions on work seen.		
14 Reflect with a partner on how to improve own created games.		
15 Suggest improvements to games – extra ways to score; how to re-start; and one main rule.		

Year 4 | Games programme

AUTUMN	SPRING	SUMMER

AUTUMN

1 Respond readily to instructions and signals and follow sensible rules of behaviour.
2 Recognise the need for safety considerations in dress and sharing of space.
3 Repeat and improve skills learned previously, showing confidence and control.
4 Start to anticipate direction of passes and try to intercept.
5 Demonstrate neat, quiet running.
6 Revise good dodging and marking footwork with quick stops and starts, changes of speed and direction, and 'fake' moves.
7 Start to mark a player, with and without the ball, and cover defensive team-mates.
8 Practise a variety of ways to send, receive and carry a ball – throw, catch, head, kick, bounce, dribble, volley.
9 Learn to 'Give and go'; 'Pass and follow'; 'Run to a space if you want to receive a pass', constantly planning ahead.
10 Demonstrate an understanding of simple skills and principles in attack and defence in invasion games, e.g. 'one on one' marking 'in line' in defence.

SPRING

1 Use vigorous leg action to keep warm on cold days and to develop heart, lungs and fitness.
2 Develop versatility in passing a ball at different heights and speeds to outwit a close marking opponent, sometimes using a 'fake'.
3 Lead and follow a partner to practise quick responses and to practise observing movement.
4 Play fairly, compete honestly, and demonstrate good sporting attitudes and behaviour.
5 Demonstrate the ability to plan and refine a performance to achieve greater efficiency.
6 Plan and play own versions of recognised team games, sometimes restricting attackers and defenders to keep the game open with more space for passing a ball.
7 Plan, use and be able to explain simple tactics to outwit an opponent.
8 Include '3 lives' games to concentrate on one thing at a time – attack or defence.
9 Use a 'fast break' on gaining possession to outrun the opponents to their goal line.
10 Make simple, helpful comments and judgements on others' performance.

SUMMER

1 Revise, practise and refine skills of net and striking/fielding games, by yourself and with others.
2 Show ability to sustain energetic activity.
3 Send a ball longer distances with an overarm throw.
4 Bowl underarm with confidence and accuracy, understanding 'good length'.
5 Apply attacking principles of hitting into space, varying direction and judging when and if to run.
6 Back one another up as fielders.
7 Plan and create your own versions of recognised games, deciding rules to keep games moving with all involved.
8 Plan and use simple tactics in a range of games and judge their effectiveness.
9 Enjoy the variety of games able to be played in warmer weather – invasion, net and striking/fielding.
10 Explore and understand common skills and principles in games – side towards ball when striking; preparatory back swing before hitting; moving early to be in position to receive.
11 Plan decisions thoughtfully.

Year 5

Games programme

AUTUMN	SPRING	SUMMER
1 Respond quickly; accept rules; wear sensible clothing.	1 Encourage good sporting behaviour when playing, refining own games, considering rules, scoring, tactics.	1 Practise to improve skills of net and striking/fielding games with a partner or small group in a games situation.
2 Send, receive and travel with a ball with increasing control and accuracy.	2 Send, receive and travel with a ball with greater confidence and control.	2 Demonstrate overarm bowling action from standing and after a run up.
3 Refine and apply dodging and marking techniques in games.	3 Show adaptability, using one- and two-handed, varied passes.	3 Field ball with confidence from varied speeds, heights, lengths, and throw in at speed.
4 Mark player with and without the ball, denying space.	4 Value good footwork in offence (side steps, quick stops, direction and speed changes) and defence (marking 'in line').	4 Demonstrate forehand and backhand volleys with confidence.
5 Develop habitual use of 'Pass and follow'; 'Give and go!'; and 'Move to receive a pass'.	5 Mark an opponent, with and without the ball, frustrating his or her movement.	5 Co-operate to make long rallies with a partner.
6 Plan ways to keep small-sided games moving and involving everyone.	6 Learn to 'screen' a ball fairly from a chasing opponent.	6 Show ability to draw partner into net by varying length of strike.
7 Collect a ball on the run with confidence and control with hands, feet or stick.	7 Experience many small-sided versions of recognised games – football, hockey, rugby, netball, basketball, as well as benchball, headingball and team passing.	7 Decide on rules, scoring, player limits to keep games flowing and involve everyone fairly.
8 Work co-operatively with team-mates to work ball from end to end.	8 Apply basic principles of attack – keep possession, support ball carrier, create space, often by keeping out of the way.	8 Condemn anti-social behaviour including unfair play.
9 In small-sided versions of recognised games, revise common skills and principles of attack and defence, e.g. quick passing 'fast break' if possible; mark 'in line' in 'one on one' defending.	9 Apply basic principles of defence – mark opponent, try interceptions, deny space.	9 Observe partner's volleying and suggest how to improve.
10 Be able to watch a team's defence or attack and comment on its effectiveness.	10 Use simple tactics like shaping a team attack to make space.	10 Experience small-sided versions of cricket, tennis, volleyball, rounders, adapting them to benefit everyone.
	11 Be able to explain a successful team or group demonstration.	11 Compare two performances and point out differences in content and effectiveness.
		12 Reflect on the physical and social benefits of a good Games programme and whole-hearted participation.

Year 6 | Games programme

AUTUMN	SPRING	SUMMER

AUTUMN

1 Dress sensibly from safety and hygiene points of view.
2 Respond readily to sensible rules and instructions.
3 Respond quickly to others' actions, planning and applying quick decision-making.
4 Understand and apply the footwork rule in games.
5 Develop versatility and variety in ways of travelling with, sending and receiving a ball.
6 Use own 'invented games' to apply skills learned in lesson.
7 Improve and use effective footwork – pivoting, changing speed and direction, dodging.
8 Understand common skills and defence e.g. 'shape' game in attack to make space; switch quickly from defence to attack; fast break, passing often, dribbling seldom; cover a defending partner.
9 Show good sporting behaviour.
10 Make positive contributions to a group in co-operative and competitive situations.
11 Plan and use simple tactics and judge their success.

SPRING

1 Achieve a high level of physical activity in all lessons and understand its effect on the body.
2 Improve skills of sending, receiving and travelling with a ball, using hands, feet and stick.
3 Sustain energetic activity to maintain winter warmth.
4 Respond quickly to a changing environment and adjust to other people's actions.
5 Experience small-sided versions of recognised games – football, netball, basketball, hockey, rugby.
6 Plan extra ways to score to make games more interesting. 'Score in either hoop, one point, or on line, two points.'
7 Use attacking principles, e.g. varied team shapes, diamond 1:2:1 or square 2:2, to spread defence to make space.
8 Understand common skills and principles in defence, e.g. marking opponent with or without ball, full court or half court, 1 on 1 defence.
9 Learn and apply the specific rules of different games.
10 Suggest ways to improve a performance by others.

SUMMER

1 Perform skills of net and striking/fielding games with increasing control and confidence.
2 Play small-sided versions of recognised games – cricket, tennis, rounders, volleyball, stoolball.
3 Be aware of varying roles and skills as a member of a team – bat, bowl, field, keep wicket, serve, backhand, forehand, volley.
4 Improve and repeat longer, more complex sequences – rallies in tennis and volleyball; flowing bowling, batting, fielding and throwing in, in cricket.
5 Show awareness of simple court positions, e.g. return to centre after each stroke.
6 Demonstrate capacity, as a class, to organise selves and get games started quickly.
7 Demonstrate accurate bowling, controlled batting, and quick off the mark fielding and quick throwing in.
8 Plan, perform and reflect on the success of own, created games, and suggest ways to improve them.
9 Work harder, enthusiastically, for longer, in a focused way with poise, control and adaptability.

Gymnastic Activities

The lesson includes varied floorwork on a clear floor, unimpeded by gymnastic apparatus, chairs, tables, trolleys or a piano, followed by varied apparatus work which covers half to two-thirds of the lesson time. The focus is on the body and helping each pupil to move neatly with control and versatility. The lessons should also be physically demanding to develop strength and suppleness.

Activities include the natural movements of running, jumping, rolling, climbing, swinging, balancing, upending, bending, stretching and twisting. Performing these movements maintains and develops the body's capacity to use them. 'What you don't use, you lose.' Traditional, popular gymnastic skills include rolls, cartwheels, handstands, headstands, rope climbing, circling on bars, balances on inverted benches, and easy vaults on to and from a low box.

Awareness of the variety and contrasts possible in movement, and learning to demonstrate them, is developed through experiencing different shapes, directions, levels, speeds and amount of force, which can all be applied to enhance and progress a performance.

The naturalness and variety of what is being taught; children's enthusiasm for movement and their energy and capacity for hard work; and the high standards of performance that the majority can achieve, all combine to make these lessons a valuable, exciting and enjoyable part of the Physical Education programme.

Suggested headings when considering progress. Does the pupil:

- dress and behave properly, work quietly, share space sensibly?

- respond quickly and enthusiastically to instructions?

- lift, carry, place, use and share apparatus safely and sensibly?

- practise hard to improve, always trying to do neat, quiet work?

- run, jump, land, roll, climb, balance and take weight on hands with confidence and control?

- use the full range of movement in the joints concerned, putting everything into the work?

- show awareness of body parts with a good feel for different actions, shapes, directions, speeds and effort?

- plan ahead thoughtfully, visualising the intended outcome?

- observe others' actions and answer questions on what was seen?

- exude an impression of confident concentration?

- participate energetically with deep breathing, perspiration and a smiling face?

- work harder for longer, demonstrating skill and versatility?

- create, practise and refine increasingly complex sequences of two, three or more smoothly linked actions which he or she is able to remember and repeat?

- stamp work with their own personality and style?

APPARATUS WORK

Apparatus work is the most important part of the lesson and one of the most exciting areas within the programme. Pupils work, almost non-stop, at natural, popular activities as they run, jump, climb, roll, balance, swing, hang, circle and upend. Three unsatisfactory systems are encountered in primary schools:

1 Apparatus is never used as teachers feel insecure and fearful of accidents. Extended floorwork frustrates the pupils who behave badly, making the teacher even less willing to use apparatus.

2 Apparatus is brought out at the start of the morning or afternoon, and left in the same place for every class. This prevents the safe teaching of floorwork and basic skills because the floor is cluttered with apparatus.

3 The apparatus is brought from a store outside the hall, or at one end of the hall, assembled, used and then returned to the remote store, every lesson. This time-consuming system, with pile-ups at doors or at the end of the room, can take up to ten minutes of the lesson time.

The recommended system for ensuring that apparatus is lifted, carried and placed in position quickly and easily needs the co-operation of all the teachers. Before lessons start in the morning or afternoon, the portable apparatus is placed around the sides and ends of the hall adjacent to where it will be used. Each group of pupils will thus only have to carry it 2–3 metres. A well-trained class can have the apparatus in place in 30 seconds. After all lessons are finished each day, as much of the apparatus as possible should remain in the hall, in corners, against or on the platform, or at the sides and ends of the room. Mats can sometimes be stored vertically behind climbing frames, benches and boxes.

ORGANISING GROUPS FOR APPARATUS WORK

Because the combinations of apparatus used in infant lessons are usually simple, such as bench and mat, or low box and mat, groups of four pupils are sufficient. Combinations used in junior school lessons are larger with, for example, ropes, benches and mats, or box, benches and mats, and groups of five or six pupils are therefore appropriate.

The organisation of the seven or eight mixed infant groups and the five or six mixed junior groups is done in the first lesson in September.

Pupils are told 'These are your groups and starting places for the apparatus.' For the four- or five-lesson development of a lesson, the same groups go to the same apparatus starting places, becoming more expert in lifting, carrying and placing it.

At the end of the apparatus work, groups return to their apparatus starting places to return the apparatus to those places round the sides and ends of the room from which it was originally carried.

POSITIONING OF APPARATUS DURING LESSONS

The teacher needs to provide:

- varied actions and varied physical demands as pupils progress from apparatus to apparatus, meeting a challenging, interesting series of settings which can include:

  a climbing and swinging on ropes

  b rolling on mats, from benches, along low box

  c balancing on inverted benches, benches, planks, box tops

  d running and jumping on to mats, across, along and from benches

  e climbing on climbing frames

  f taking weight on hands on mats, benches, planks, low boxes

  g jumping and landing from a height from a bench or box

  h circling or hanging from metal pole between trestles

  i lying and pulling along a bench or down an inclined plank

- opportunities to transfer floorwork actions and lesson themes to apparatus by providing, for example:

  a many surfaces for 'Travelling on feet and hands' – such as mats, benches, trestles and horizontal planks, trestles and inclined planks, low boxes, climbing frames

  b sufficient floor space around the apparatus to permit 'Good use of space, particularly directions' or 'Sequences, starting and finishing on the surrounding floor space'

  c a variety of challenging surfaces for 'Balance', with low mats, benches and inverted benches; medium height box tops, planks between trestles; high planks and metal pole between trestles; inclined planks; and vertical climbing frame

- a safe environment by ensuring:

  a mats are in place where pupils are expected to land from a height

  b mats are well away from walls, windows, doors or other obstacles such as a piano, trolleys or chairs, and well away from the landing areas of adjacent apparatus

  c mats are in position under high planks or poles between trestles where pupils are hanging under or circling around

  d height and width of apparatus are appropriate for the age of the class – not too narrow to balance on; not too high to jump down or roll from

SAFE, CO-OPERATIVE HANDLING OF APPARATUS

Having organised the groupings for apparatus during the first lesson of the year, the teacher should teach and practise the lifting, carrying and putting in place of the apparatus as follows.

Infants

The typical spread of eight or nine, simple sets of apparatus around the sides and ends of the room might include:

- bench and mat

- trestle, inclined plank and mat

- ropes frame

- 18in nesting table and mat

- bottom section of box and mat

- bench and mat

- two trestles, plank to link trestles and mat

- climbing frame

- top section of two-section box and mat.

Two pupils stand at the ropes and two stand at the climbing frames. At all other positions there are four pupils.

The teacher asks the class – 'Sit beside your apparatus and watch carefully.' He or she goes to a bench and mat group and tells the four pupils to stand 'One at each side and one at each end. Bend your knees, put your hands under your side of the bench with arms straight. Stand up and and lift carefully. Carry it to here, please, then bend your knees to put it down quietly.' The teacher shows them a position, 2–3 metres from where they started. 'Jim and Susan, please bring your mat and put it beside the bench.' Then, 'Well done, this group. You can sit down now.'

A confident teacher can now ask 'Will the other groups at a bench, a box or a nesting table, please stand with one at each end and one at each side of your apparatus. I will come to each group in turn and show you where to place your apparatus.'

The trestle, inclined plank and mat, and the pair of trestles, plank and mat groups are each shown how two pupils carry a trestle between them by facing each other in the space under the inverted 'V'. The importance of securing the hooks at the ends of the planks over a bar of the trestle is emphasised and demonstrated. Two pupils carry a plank near its ends so that the placing of the hooks over a bar of the trestle is accurate.

The teacher then shows the pair at the ropes how to operate the pulley rope to bring out climbing ropes if they are on an overhead trackway. If the ropes are on a frame which has to be wheeled out, the teacher helps the two pupils walk backwards, pulling the operating handle. Once in position, the ropes are secured when the operating handle is lifted to let the bolt on the frame enter the small socket in the floor.

The climbing frame is always wheeled out to position, pulled by an operating handle on each of the two frames. The bolts go into floor sockets, as with the ropes frame. In addition, tension wires running from frame to frame, and from frames to wall, are operated by a handle on the frame, and need to be pulled tight and secured by the teacher.

Groups are then asked to show travelling activities on the floor and up to, on to, along and from all pieces of apparatus, 'using feet only' or 'using hands and feet', for example.

Finally, the infant class is asked – 'Please go and stand beside the apparatus you brought out.' Group by group they are reminded 'One at each end, one at each side. Bend your knees, lift and carry it back to the side of the room where it came from.' Trestles, ropes and climbing frame groups are also given a reminder and helped to put their apparatus away 'sensibly and carefully'.

Groups are praised for 'the quiet, safe and sensible way you all moved your apparatus,' and told 'Please remember your starting places for apparatus for next week.'

Juniors

In their first lesson, Year 3 should be reminded of the correct, safe way to lift, carry and place their starting apparatus, in case they come from a school where pupils did not do so.

A typical spread of five or six sets of apparatus around the sides and ends of the hall might include:

- ropes and two mats
- four mats
- two benches and two mats
- climbing frames
- two boxes, one bench and two mats
- five trestles, two planks, one pole and three mats.

There are five or six pupils in each group. Pairs can be shown how to 'Stand at opposite ends of your bench or box. Bend your knees, grip under your side with arms straight, and stand and carry it to the place I show you,' which will be nearby.

Individuals carry the trestles, planks and pole and co-operate in linking them as requested by the teacher. Pairs carry mats to place under planks and pole. Ropes and climbing frames are brought out by individuals, assisted by the teacher.

The class then uses the apparatus with simple challenges which might include 'Travel on to, along and from all apparatus and think of the varied actions it is possible to include.'

To finish, the class are asked to 'Please go and stand beside the apparatus you brought out.' Group by group, with the teacher nearby, they lift, carry and return their apparatus to its starting place.

Groups are praised for their 'safe and sensible handling of apparatus' and asked to 'Please remember your starting places for the next lesson.'

Mats are used to cushion a landing from a height and to roll on. We do not need mats under ropes or around climbing frames because we do not ask pupils to jump down from a height. If mats are placed around climbing frames, pupils often behave in a foolhardy way, enticed into dangerous jumping.

THREE WAYS TO TEACH APPARATUS WORK

1 **Pupils use all the apparatus freely, as they respond to tasks that relate to the lesson theme**. Several challenges provide non-stop apparatus work for infants and juniors; pupils are stationary only when watching a demonstration, having a teaching point emphasised, or when being given the next task.

This method is particularly popular with infant classes because they are able to visit and use all pieces of apparatus, including their favourites – ropes and climbing frames.

'Show me a still balance and beautifully stretched body shape on each piece of apparatus.' (Balance and body shape awareness)

'Show me how you can approach each piece of apparatus going forward, and leave going sideways.' (Space awareness – directions)

'Leader, show your partner one touch only on each piece of apparatus, then off to the next piece.' (Partner work)

2 **Groups stay and work at one set of apparatus**. Repetition helps pupils improve and remember a series of linked actions. The task is the same for all groups, based on the lesson theme.

'Make your hands important in arriving on, and feet important in leaving the apparatus.' (Body part awareness)

'Can you include swings on to and off apparatus; a swing into a roll; and a swing to take all weight on your hands?' (Swinging)

'Travel from opposite sides, up to, on, along and from the apparatus, to finish in your partner's starting place.' (Partner work)

Groups rotate to the next apparatus after about five minutes.

3 **Each group practises a different, specific skill on each set of apparatus – balancing, rolling, climbing, for example.** This method of teaching is more difficult than the other two because it needs more technical knowledge and because the teacher is giving out five or six sets of instructions instead of one. As it is a direct challenge to 'skills hungry' pupils it is very popular.

Benches 'At upturned benches, slowly balance walk forward. Look straight ahead. Feel for the bench before you step on it.'

Ropes 'Grip strongly with hands together and feet crossed. Can you take one hand off, while swinging, to prove a good foot grip?'

Low cross box 'A face vault is like a high bunny jump to cross the box, as you twist over, facing the box top all the way.'

Climbing frames 'Travel by moving hands only, then feet only.'

Mats 'Roll sideways with body curled small, and with body long and stretched' – log roll.

Groups rotate to the next apparatus after about five minutes.

RETURN ACTIVITIES IN APPARATUS WORK

Whichever method of teaching apparatus work is used, pupils will be encouraged to 'Be found working, not waiting.' Most waiting in apparatus work is caused by groups queuing to come on to a bench, box, trestle or mat, when only one group member is working at a time.

By including return activities rather than queuing, the pupils in the following groups:

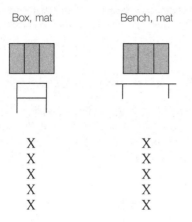

Box, mat   Bench, mat

X   X
X   X
X   X
X   X
X   X

can enjoy up to five times as much involvement, as follows:

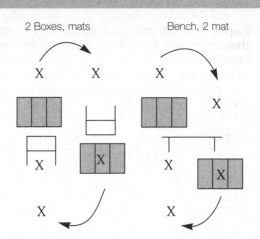

2 Boxes, mats   Bench, 2 mat

When they are about to move to a new apparatus position, pupils are told, 'When you arrive at your next apparatus place, space yourselves so that everyone can start on my signal. Some can stand at the usual starting positions, others will stand on the mats as if you have just finished, and others might be on the apparatus as if half-way through the activity. Change now, please.'

When they are standing at the next apparatus, the teacher checks that there are no queues and that everyone has room to begin on the signal 'Start now, please.'

SIMPLE, TRADITIONAL, POPULAR GYMNASTIC SKILLS

Roll forward across mat. Crouch, feet apart, hands shoulder width apart. Lean forward, weight on hands, tucking head well under to contact with floor with the back of the head and neck. Leg push and curled body help the roll. Bend knees at the end to a crouch, helped by reaching arms forward, eventually to standing.

Roll backward from sitting, knees bent. Arms are fully bent with elbows close to sides. Wrists are bent backward and palms of hands face upward, thumbs towards ears. Roll along back, shoulders, and bottom of neck. A strong hand push from the floor and a high lift of hips over the head takes body back over the head to land on feet which have been brought down as near hands as possible.

Roll sideways (a) from kneeling with one leg stretched sideways. Roll away from extended leg, tucking chin on to chest, or (b) from back, lying with body stretched with arms straight above head or down at sides (log roll). Impetus for roll is a swing across from the opposite shoulder, or opposite hip and leg, or (c) from back, lying with body curled tightly. Momentum for roll can be from a small rock to the left, rock to right, then roll right over to the left and on to the back again.

Cartwheel, ideally practised along a line of floorboards. Left hand on floor to left side in line with feet. Right hand on floor about half a metre from the left hand and in line with feet. Jump off both feet and land on the right foot beyond right hand, in line with hands. Push with hands to stretch up, turn body and put left foot in an astride position. 'Left, right, right, left' of hand, hand, foot, foot along a line.

Bunny jump Crouch with hands on floor, a shoulder width apart, fingers spread and pointing forwards. Arms are straight, head looks ahead. One or two little bounces take the weight briefly on hands, then a bigger bounce takes and holds all weight on hands. Bent legs help to lift hips above shoulders and hands – the position required.

Handstand Follows much practice of bunny jumps and being upended. From standing, with arms above head, a step is taken, placing hands flat on floor shoulder width apart with fingers pointing forwards. The back leg swings up straight with weight over shoulders, arms straight. The second leg swings up beside leading leg. A stretched body with straight legs above shoulders and hands is the target.

Bent leg headstand From a kneeling starting position, place hands on the mat shoulder width apart, pointing forwards, forming a triangle. Knees are lifted and the gymnast walks forward on tiptoes until hips are near vertical. With feet together, bent knees are levered up to headstand position. Bent legs makes balance easier than a full, straight-legged headstand.

Elbow balance from a crouch start with feet apart, hands on floor, fingers forward and a little less than shoulder width apart. Bend elbows to place them inside and under knees. Tilt body forward, slowly, from feet on to hands, until toes come a short distance off the floor.

Rope climbing (a) stand, holding rope with hands together, arms high. Swing, gripping rope between sole of one foot and instep of the other. Feel the importance of a strong, crossed foot grip, or (b) swing with a strong, crossed foot grip secure enough to let you take one hand from the rope,

without sliding down with other hand, or (c) climb, using three hand shifts for every lift of feet – 'One hand up and grip; other hand up and grip; first hand up and grip just above second hand. Now pull legs up and grip strongly with crossed feet.' 'Hand, hand, hands together, feet up.'

Downward circle on metal pole or bar of climbing frame. Body is balanced on top of thighs on pole or bar. Thumbs are placed on top, pointing forward, fingers are under and pointing back.

1 Bend arms and hips to let waist rest on bar or pole.

2 Curl slowly round bar or pole until bent knees come under it.

3 Lower feet, slowly, to floor and stand up.

Balance standing on upturned bench, one foot in front of the other. Practise little knee bends with arms sideways to help balance. Eyes look straight ahead, not down.

Balance walk forward on inverted bench. Leading foot feels the side of the supporting surface, then feels for the top of the supporting surface before putting weight down. Head and eyes are kept steady, looking forward at head height, never down. Parts of both feet are in contact with bench at all times.

Balance walk backward on inverted bench. Leading foot feels its way back, along side of supporting surface, then feels for top of the supporting surface before putting its weight down. Parts of both feet are in contact with bench at all times.

'Cat walk' balance along inverted bench. Crouch on top surface, one foot in front of the other, with weight evenly shared between hands and feet. Knees are well bent and hips are low. Use slow, small steps in a crawling action.

Face vault is a high bunny jump over a low, cross box. Approach at right angles and place hands obliquely on top of box. With a two-footed take-off, spring up and over box with bottom well up and over hands. Head is well up and knees are kept bent. Hands stay on top of box until feet, together, reach mat. Eyes 'face' the box all the way.

Squat jump is used to bring you on to a bench or a low box, as a preliminary to a second activity taking you from the bench or box. Hands are placed shoulder width apart on apparatus, from a standing start or after a run up. A two-footed push lifts you through a 'bunny jump' position to being crouched, with feet between hands, on bench or box. The gymnast can spring up and jump from box or bench; roll along box or from bench; stand and cartwheel along box or down from bench; lie and pull along bench.

THE LESSON PLAN

One answer to the question 'What do we teach in a Gymnastic Activities lesson?' might be – 'All the natural actions and ways of moving of which the body is capable and which, if practised whole-heartedly and safely, ensure normal, healthy growth and physical development!'

It has been said that 'What you don't use, you lose.' Most pupils nowadays seldom strenuously use their natural capacity for vigorous running, jumping and landing from a height; rolling in different directions; balancing on a variety of body parts; upending to take their weight on their hands; gripping, climbing and swinging on a rope; hanging, swinging and circling on a bar; or whole body bending, stretching, arching and twisting.

These natural movements and actions should be present in every Gymnastic Activities lesson, ensuring that pupils do not lose the ability to do them and have their physical development diminished.

A class teacher's determination to inspire the class to use and not lose their natural physicality can be strengthened by looking at the cars queuing as near to the school exit as possible, to transport children home, with the minimum of walking, to their after school, house-bound, sedentary inaction.

Floorwork starts the lesson and includes:

a Activities for the legs, exploring and developing the many actions possible when travelling on feet, and ways to jump and land.

b Activities for the body, including the many ways to bend, stretch, rock, roll, arch, twist, curl, turn, and the ways in which body parts receive, support and transfer the body weight in travelling and balancing.

c Activities for the arms and shoulders, the least used parts of our body. We strengthen them by using them to hold all or part of the body weight on the spot or moving. This strength is needed in gripping, climbing, hanging, swinging and circling, and in levering on to and across apparatus, supported by the hands only.

Apparatus work is the climax of the lesson, making varied, unique and challenging physical demands of pupils whose whole body – legs, arms and shoulders, back and abdominals – has to work strongly because of the more difficult:

• travelling on hands and feet, over, under, across and around obstacles, as well as vertically, often supported only by the hands

• jumping and landing from greater heights

• rolling on to, along, from and across apparatus

• balancing on high or narrow surfaces

• upending to take all body weight on hands on apparatus above floor level

• gripping, swinging, climbing and circling on ropes and bars.

OBSERVING A GYMNASTIC ACTIVITIES LESSON

The Hall

a Clean floor?

b Satisfactory temperature?

c Safe, with no intrusive, dangerous piano, chairs, tables, trolley?

d Clear floor sockets for securing bolts of frames and ropes?

The Class

a Safely and sensibly dressed – no watches, rings, long sleeves or trousers, unbunched long hair, socks without shoes?

b Well-behaved – no uninvited talking; instant responses to instructions; sharing floor and apparatus unselfishly; attentive, interested observers of demonstrations; sensible and co-operative in lifting, carrying and placing apparatus safely?

The Teacher

a Sensibly dressed for a 'physical' lesson, with appropriate footwear, at least, as an example to the class?

b Is there a lesson plan as a reminder of the lesson's content?

General Impression

a Is the hall – 'A scene of busy activity with everyone being found to be working, not waiting', almost all of the time?

b Are deep breathing, perspiration and smiling faces evident to prove that pupils are working vigorously and wholeheartedly at a variety of activities which they are enjoying?

The Teaching

a Is the class 'put in the picture' regarding the lesson's main aim, emphasis or theme?

b Are opportunities being provided for planning the activities? 'Can you plan a short sequence of some of your favourite balances?'

c Are opportunities being provided for reflecting on and evaluating work observed, or performed by self? 'What three very neat travelling actions did Susan demonstrate?'

d Are 'dead spots', when no-one is working, being kept to a minimum? Or are lessons interrupted by:
  • over-long instructions and explanations
  • too many demonstrations
  • too many, long-winded reflections?

Apparatus

a Placed around sides and ends of the hall, near to where it will be positioned and used?

b Brought out and put away 'Quietly, carefully and sensibly'?

Does the lesson include a satisfactory conclusion? Praise? Thanks? Is there a relaxed and calm atmosphere?

Reception

Emphasis on *(a)* planning and practising to link two or more actions together; *(b)* demonstrating greater confidence through neat controlled work.

FLOORWORK – 12 minutes

Legs

1 Can you do an upward jump where you are, then show me a short run and another high jump?

2 In each jump, can you stretch your whole body beautifully?

3 Let your knees 'give' softly and quietly when you land.

Body

1 Show me a favourite body shape (stretched, arched, wide, curled, twisted or bridge-like).

2 Move to a new body part and show me a different shape.

3 Try to make a little sequence of three changing shapes you can remember and repeat.

Arms

1 Put your hands on the floor and show me two or three ways to lift your feet off the floor, putting them down quietly in a different place.

2 You can lift them and put them down on the same spot, or twist to one side, or lift the feet to go forward, outside or between your hands.

APPARATUS WORK – 16 minutes

1 Travel up to, and on to a piece of apparatus and show me a still, strong body shape. Leave the apparatus and travel to a new floor space, standing beautifully stretched. (Repeat up to and on to the next piece of apparatus.)

2 From your own floor space, can you make your hands important as you travel up to, on to, along and from each piece of apparatus?

3 Keep both arms straight and strong as you put your hands only on the apparatus. Lift bent legs off the floor to take all the weight on your hands. You can put your feet down on the same spot or in a new one (e.g. to cross a bench).

4 Can you stay at the piece of apparatus where you are now, and be very clever, by joining together for me:

a a still, stretched, balanced starting position
b your way of travelling up to and on to the apparatus, using feet or feet and hands
c a still position on the apparatus with a clear, body shape
d a neat, still, finishing position, away from apparatus, on the floor.

FINAL FLOOR ACTIVITY – 2 minutes

Can you run and jump high, then run and jump long?

Year 1

Emphasis on *(a)* working harder for longer, linking two or more simple actions to plan and create sequences; *(b)* demonstrating an expanding repertoire of neat movements.

FLOORWORK – 12 minutes

Legs

1 Show me a short sequence of your favourite ways to travel, using feet only. Use a still start and finish each time.

2 Can you name your two or three actions?

3 Include different actions (not always running and jumping) performed in a variety of ways (e.g. using different directions, shapes, speeds).

Body

1 Can you join two or three arched, bridge-like shapes?

2 This shape will have three or four sides, where the floor is usually one of the sides.

3 Try a high-level bridge, like standing with upper body reaching down; a medium bridge, like a crab; and a low bridge, where you might be lying, arched from shoulders to waist.

Arms

1 Plan an interesting pathway as you travel on hands and feet.

2 You can go forward and back to the same place, or round three sides of a triangle, or four sides of a square.

3 Variety and contrast, which are good to see, can come from a change of direction, shape or level.

APPARATUS WORK – 16 minutes

1 Travel to the nearest apparatus using feet only. Travel on to and along it, using hands and feet. Perform a bridge-like shape on your apparatus. Leave the apparatus and return to a still finish position on the floor. Practise this sequence at the same place several times so that you can remember and improve it.

2 Show me a jump and a 'squashy' landing somewhere. It can be on a mat before you go on to apparatus, or it can be your way of leaving the apparatus. You might even include a sideways roll after your jump.

3 All move to a new piece of apparatus and stand ready. Practise again and show me your best still start and finish, your bridge, and your jumping and landing. Stay on the apparatus and practise to improve.

4 I am looking for neat, quiet, well-controlled actions, good body shapes, and a change of direction or level somewhere for variety and contrast.

FINAL FLOOR ACTIVITY – 2 minutes

Using your feet only, show me a still, well stretched balance. Travel a few steps into a different balance. Travel to a third, different balance.

Year 2

Emphasis on *(a)* partner work, with its enjoyable and co-operative experiences; *(b)* working hard to achieve success.

FLOORWORK – 12 minutes

Legs

1 One partner practises a simple, repeating pattern of walking, running, jumping or skipping in their own floor space. The other partner practises a pattern in the whole floor space.

2 Each show your sequence to your partner, once or twice, so that your partner can remember it.

3 Can you now perform together, doing the on the spot pattern, then the pattern using the whole floor space?

Body

1 Stand, facing each other, and slowly build up a pattern of whole body movements, taking turns to decide the next one. I am looking for big body stretches, long and wide, and curls, twists and arching.

2 Work slowly so that you can mirror each other. Do two movements, then repeat, improve and remember them before going on to a third movement.

3 Are you showing variety (e.g. changing direction or level) or contrast (e.g. a sudden change of speed)?

Arms

1 Follow your leader, travelling slowly on hands and feet.

2 Leader, can you include a direction change?

3 Other partner, become the new leader and keep working at the same sequence. Can you change it slightly by making a different body part lead (not always the head, for example)?

APPARATUS WORK – 16 minutes

1 One leading, one following, travel up to each group of apparatus and travel on it. Return to your starting place and start again.

2 This time, as you follow each other on the apparatus, try to show me good support on hands and feet, with some interesting big body movements like you used together in the floorwork.

3 Start on opposite sides of your piece of apparatus and try:

a partner A shows the leg activity pattern from the start of the floorwork, in own space

b partner B copies and then travels up to the apparatus, using leg activity actions from the floorwork

c partner A travels, copying, up to the apparatus

d slowly, agreeing who is leader, they pass each other with an identical action, and

e travel freely to finish in partner's starting position.

FINAL FLOOR ACTIVITY – 2 minutes

Partner A leads a simple travelling pattern along straight lines. Partner B leads a pattern of travelling along curving lines.

Year 3

Theme Jumping, rolling, balancing

FLOORWORK – 12 minutes

Legs

1 Do small jumps where you are. Keep your body straight, but let your knees bend to make the landing soft and quiet.

2 After a short run, jump up from one or both feet. Show me a nice, 'squashy' landing, with a good bend in your knees and ankles.

3 Use stretched arms to help you balance on landing. Arms can stretch forward or sideways.

Body

1 Lie on your back, curled up small. Roll back and forwards from your bottom all the way to your shoulders and hands.

2 Now, with hands clasped under knees, still curled up on your back, can you roll from side to side?

3 Can you start, crouched; lower into a roll back and forward; roll from side to side; then rock back and strongly forward up on to your feet?

Arms

1 With a long swing of arms from above your head, can you try to balance in a handstand?

2 Try an elbow balance. From a crouch position, place hands on the floor, elbows slightly bent and inside and under knees. Tilt body weight forward from the feet on to the hands.

APPARATUS WORK – 16 minutes

1 As you travel all round the room without touching apparatus, can you include jumps across mats, over benches and low planks?

2 When I call 'Stop!' show me a balance on the nearest piece of apparatus, or apparatus and floor.

3 Travel freely on the floor and apparatus. You may roll on mats, and from apparatus (e.g. from sitting, kneeling, lying on benches, planks or low box tops). With a nicely stretched body, can you jump off the apparatus, land softly, and lower into a smooth sideways roll?

4 Now stay at your present apparatus places to practise, repeat and improve the following:

a start and finish on the floor, away from the apparatus

b travel up to, on, along and away from your apparatus and show me

c jumps, rolls, and a beautifully still balance with a clear body shape.

FINAL FLOOR ACTIVITY – 2 minutes

Balance on tiptoes with arms stretched to help balance. Run, jump and land with a balanced finish, helped by straight arms again.

Year 4

Theme Awareness of body parts, feeling and understanding how the body works in its many ways of supporting, receiving and transferring the body weight.

FLOORWORK – 12–15 minutes

Legs

1 Practise soft, quiet jumps on the spot. Stretch ankles and knees at take-off and let them 'give' gently on landing.

2 Skip round the room using the same good stretch in the pushing ankle. Let the leg in the air travel high forward with its ankle well stretched and the opposite arm reaching forward as a balance. (Opposite arm and thigh horizontal.)

Body

1 Stand with feet apart. Slowly bend down, leading with your head. Neck joints, shoulders, back, waist, hips, knees and ankles all 'give' until you are crouched down low.

2 Rise up in the opposite order, stretching ankles, knees, hips, waist, back, shoulders, neck and finish by stretching arms above head.

3 Repeat, feeling the order in which joints close and open.

Arms

1 Travel slowly on hands and feet, in and out of the other members of the class.

2 Keep arms and legs straight for a strong movement.

3 Can you move arms only, then legs only?

4 Bouncing is a strong action, springing everything up off the floor.

APPARATUS WORK – 16–18 minutes

1 Travel round, touching only the mats and the floor. When I call 'Stop!', quickly find a place on the nearest apparatus, with both feet off the apparatus and ankles stretched strongly.

2 When I stop you next time, show me a fully stretched body on a piece of apparatus. Stop! Now, slowly curl into a rounded shape.

3 Next time, stretch a different body part on a different piece of apparatus. Stop! Slowly curl everything in.

4 Walk to many pieces of apparatus and try out the ways in which your hands can lift, lever, jump, circle or twist you on to apparatus.

5 Stay at your starting apparatus places and work hard to feel how the body parts work to receive, support and transfer your body weight on, across, under, around and from the apparatus.

Mats – rolling
Climbing frames – climbing
Ropes – swinging or climbing
Trestles, poles, planks – travelling
Upturned benches, mats – balancing
Box, bench, mats – running and jumping, rolling, weight on hands

FINAL FLOOR ACTIVITY – 2 minutes

Can you make different body parts lead when travelling (knees, head, elbow, toes, side, etc.)?

Year 5

Theme Direct teaching of simple, traditional gymnastic skills.

FLOORWORK – 13–16 minutes

Legs

1 Jump on the spot with a good stretch of whole body in the air, particularly the ankle joints.

2 Practise three of these skip jumps, followed by a tuck jump where knees are pulled up as high as possible.

3 Do four skip jumps followed by jumping with the feet astride then together, twice.

Body

Ski swings. With the feet apart, swing arms forward and upward above the head. Swing arms down past sides, then up above head to a high stretch. Long arm swing down and back, with full knee bend, then swing arms upward and stretch knees. Long arm swing down and back, with full knee bend, then swing arms upward and stretch the knees. Lower arms and repeat.

Arms

Elbow balance, with only hands on floor. Crouch with feet apart and hands under shoulders. Bend elbows slightly to place them inside and under knees. Tilt body forward, from feet on to hands, until toes come off the floor and you are balancing on hands only.

APPARATUS WORK – 17–19 minutes

Mats

1 Forward roll; stand up with one foot crossed behind the other; twist the body half round to side of rear foot; finish with a backward roll.

2 Log roll sideways with body straight, arms stretched above head.

Climbing Frames

1 Travel vertically up, diagonally down.

2 With a partner, start at opposite bottom corners. Climb to top corner and come down diagonally, passing at the centre.

Ropes

1 Swing with hands together and crossed foot grip. As you swing, can you take one hand off to prove a good foot grip?

Low, long box, cross box, mats

Catspring using hands and feet on to the near end of the long box. Either cartwheel, roll or bunny jump along and from the box. At the cross box, face vault across on both hands, like high bunny jumping, facing the box top all the way.

Upturned benches

1 Balance walk forwards. Leading foot feels its way alongside the side of the supporting surface. Moving foot feels for the balancing surface before putting weight down on itself, i.e. parts of both feet always maintain contact with the bench.

2 When you feel confident enough, try walking backwards.

Year 6

Theme Sequences through which the pupils work harder for longer, expressing vigour, skilfulness, understanding and, it is hoped, enthusiasm, enjoyment and satisfaction.

FLOORWORK – 12–15 minutes

Legs

Show me a sequence where you work on the spot to start with, then travel to a new space of your own. Can you plan to include more than one kind of leg action, and examples of both gentle and vigorous movements?

Body

Can you travel using stretching and curling movements? Working at different levels, using different supporting parts of the body will provide interesting variety.

Arms

Travel, using feet and hands, and emphasise the varied pattern of possible foot and hand movements. They can move alternately; left side only, right side only; apart or together; or run and cartwheel or handstand, etc.

APPARATUS WORK – 16–18 minutes

Climbing Frames

1 Using floor and apparatus, can you balance, travel, balance, using a variety of supporting body parts in your balances?

2 Can you plan to include a vertical, horizontal and upended position?

Ropes

1 In your climbing, emphasise the full stretch after the three-count hand shift, and the full curl after the high legs lift.

2 Show me a sequence of three swings that include a change of direction and body shape.

Inverted Benches, mats

In your balancing along the benches, travel at different levels and include a change of direction somewhere. At the mats, revise elbow balance and/or bent leg headstand.

Boxes, mats

Can you include a rolling action along the low, long box and mats? Show me a vaulting action on the cross box with shoulders over hands on the return. Try to plan for a long, flowing sequence.

Trestles, planks, pole, mats

Can you travel, using all the apparatus, with feet leading or following on, under, across, around and along the apparatus?

Mats

Show me a balance, roll, balance sequence where you include at least one upended balance and a change of direction somewhere. At the return mats, can you do a forward roll followed by a dive forward roll (i.e. whole of body in air at one point)?

FINAL FLOOR ACTIVITY – 2 minutes

Make a sequence using walking, running and jumping which includes varied actions in flight, for example hurdling, jackknife, scissors, tuck, rolling one leg over the other.

PROGRESSING A GYMNASTIC ACTIVITIES LESSON OVER 4 OR 5 LESSONS

USING 'STEPPING' AS AN EXAMPLE

Lesson 1

a **Concentrate on the 'what?'**, the actions, their correct form, and how the body parts concerned are working. 'Can you step quietly and neatly, visiting all parts of the room? Travel along straight lines, never following anyone.' 'Can you vary the idea of "stepping", not always passing your feet?' (Chasse, crossover, toes down and swing, skips, hops, bounces etc.)

b **Insist on good, clear body shapes** to make everything look better, and be more demanding. 'Step out nice and tall. Show me clear arms, legs and body shape. Are you long and stretched or is there a shape change somewhere?'

Lesson 2

Concentrate on the 'where?' of the movements, adding variety and quality to the work by good use, of own and whole room floor space, directions and levels. 'Can you sometimes step on the spot (particularly when you are in a crowded area) and sometimes use the whole room space – sides, corners, ends, as well as the middle?' 'Stepping actions sideways and backwards are interesting – sliding; stepping-closing (chasse); or stepping-crossing over; as well as feet passing normally. The leading leg can swing in many directions.'

Lesson 3

Concentrate on the 'how?' of the movements and the way that changes in speed and effort (force) might make the work look more controlled and neat, as well as giving them greater variety, contrast and interest. 'Can you include a change of speed in your stepping? This is interesting if a change of direction accompanies the speed change. Side, side, slow, slow; forward quick, forward, quick.' 'Can you make parts of your stepping small, quiet, soft, and make other parts bigger, firmer and stronger?' (On the spot, keep it soft, 1, 2, 3, 4; on the move, big, strong strides, 1, 2, 3, 4.)

Lesson 4/Lessons 4 and 5

Ask for sequences that draw together all the practising, learning, adapting and remembering that have taken place during the previous lessons. Aim for almost non-stop action, working harder for longer with enthusiasm, understanding and concentration.

'In your three- or four-part stepping sequence, can you include:

a varied stepping actions with good, firm, poised body shapes

b interesting and varied use of space

c a change of speed or force somewhere?'

Infant

LESSON 1 OF A 4-LESSON DEVELOPMENT

Theme (a) Planning and performing simple skills safely; (b) body shape awareness.
Concentrating on (a) the 'what?', the actions and how the body parts work to perform them neatly; (b) good, clear body shapes to make the body work hard and make the work look neat and well-controlled.

FLOORWORK – 12 minutes

Legs

1 Can you run a few steps, jump up high to show me a good body shape in the air, then do a soft, squashy landing?

2 Try a long, stretched shape with arms high above your head.

3 Stretched arms and legs can be together for an arrow shape or stretched wide like a star. Try both ways.

Body

1 Stand, balanced tall on tiptoes. Stretch arms forward or to the sides to help you balance.

2 Lift one foot off the floor and show me a new balance. What strong body shape are you using to keep nice and still?

3 Lower to sitting, and roll back on to your shoulders to balance in a small, curled up shape.

4 Now roll forward, right up to standing again, tall and stretched on tiptoes, ready to start again.

Arms

1 Travel slowly on hands and feet. Show me a long, wide or curled up shape as you travel, looking for spaces.

2 Your head, your feet or one side of your body can go first.

3 Can you go from a curled to a new shape as you travel?

4 Straight arms travelling is hard work, can you try it?

APPARATUS WORK – 16 minutes

1 Travel all round the room without touching any apparatus. When I call 'Stop!' show me a good shape on the nearest apparatus.

2 Stop! Make your whole body wide, curled, twisted or arched.

3 Go on to apparatus now and find places where you can show me different body shapes (e.g. stretched hanging on ropes; wide standing on box; curled lying on mat or bench; arched over bench).

4 Remember the ways you travelled on hands and feet? Can you do some of those actions slowly and carefully, using the apparatus?

5 Show me how you can travel on apparatus and hold a balance somewhere. Then do a nicely stretched jump up and off, followed by a soft, squashy landing.

6 Keep going, travelling and balancing on many pieces of apparatus. Can you use different parts of your body to balance on?

FINAL FLOOR ACTIVITY – 2 minutes

After a little run, show me a jump up with arms and legs stretched long like an arrow or wide like a star.

Infant

LESSON 2 OF A 4-LESSON DEVELOPMENT

Theme *(a)* Planning and performing simple skills safely; *(b)* body shape awareness.
Concentrating on *(a)* revising the actions and good uses of body parts from lesson 1; *(b)* revising the clear body shapes to make movements look better; *(c)* the 'where?', and how we can use our own personal space, the whole room, shared space, and different levels and directions.

FLOORWORK – 12 minutes

Legs

1 Run and jump high into a space near you, and show me a clear body shape in the air. Do a soft, 'squashy' landing.

2 Stand and show me a long, stretched shape. Now stand with legs and arms stretched wide. These two shapes are ideas for you to try as you run and jump high, now.

3 Well done. Can you think of any other shapes you can do in the air? (Look for and comment on bent tucks and twists.)

Body

1 Balance on tiptoes with stretched arms helping your balance. No wobbling! Slowly lift one foot off the floor.

2 Lower to sitting and stretch arms and legs as you balance on your bottom. Stay still!

3 Curl up tight and roll back and up on to shoulders.

4 Roll all the way back to your starting, standing, high level balance on tiptoes, ready to start again.

Arms

1 Show me slow travelling on hands and feet, with a long, wide or curled shape, or changing shapes as you travel.

2 Hands and feet can be wide apart or near. They can all move together, or hands only then feet only.

3 Can you sometimes travel sideways with one side going first, or even backward with feet going first?

APPARATUS WORK – 16 minutes

1 Run to all parts of the room without touching apparatus. When I call 'Stop!' show me a good shape, balancing on the nearest apparatus.

2 Stop! Make your body long, wide, twisted, curled or arched like a bridge. Be still. Balances can be high, medium or low level.

3 When I stop you next time, balance, still, on a different part of your body, maybe at a different level for variety. Stop!

4 Go on to and travel on the apparatus, using hands and feet, maybe using some of the actions we practised earlier in floorwork.

5 If you jump down, do a 'squashy' landing by bending the knees.

6 Travel up to and away from the apparatus with neat, quiet feet; use hands and feet to travel at different levels on apparatus, and include a still balance with a good shape.

FINAL FLOOR ACTIVITY – 2 minutes

Run for three or four steps only, then jump up high with arms and legs stretched long like an arrow or wide like a star.

Infant

LESSON 3 OF A 4-LESSON DEVELOPMENT

Theme *(a)* Planning and performing simple skills safely; *(b)* body shape awareness.
Concentrating on *(a)* revising actions, good use of body parts, and neat body shapes; *(b)* making good use of space to bring variety to the work; *(c)* the 'how?', and using varied force and speed to improve the quality and appearance of the work.

FLOORWORK – 12 minutes

Legs

1 Run a few steps, slowly, into a lively high jump with a neat body shape.

2 Land softly with 'squashy' knees and ankles, slowing you down gently.

3 Use your whole body in your beautiful shape in the air.

4 Look for a good space to run into each time you jump. Keep going.

Body

1 Balance on tiptoes and feel your body strong and firm.

2 Lift one foot off the floor and balance, firm again.

3 Relax your whole body and slowly sit down, balancing with arms and legs stretched wide. No wobbling!

4 Curl up and roll smoothly back on to your shoulders.

5 Do a quick roll forward, right up high on to both feet.

6 Be still, feeling strong and well stretched on tiptoes.

Arms

1 As you space out sensibly and travel to all parts of the room, let me see slow, strong actions.

2 Two or three actions would be good. What are your hands and feet doing? Are they wide apart or close together as you travel?

3 As you travel in different directions, different body parts can lead. Which is leading (head, feet, a side)?

APPARATUS WORK – 16 minutes

1 Use your feet softly as you travel to all parts of the room.

2 When I call 'Stop!', very quickly show me a firm body shape on the apparatus. Stop! Feel your whole body strong and firm.

3 Travel again, listening for my signal. Next time, balance on a different body part, maybe at a different level. Stop!

4 Show me your best balance, feeling your body firm and strong.

5 Travel on apparatus, using your hands and feet as you did earlier in the lesson. If you want, do a jump down with a soft landing.

6 Show me *(a)* neat travelling up to and away from apparatus, *(b)* travelling on apparatus using hands and feet, and *(c)* holding a still, firm balance somewhere on the apparatus.

FINAL FLOOR ACTIVITY – 2 minutes

Run into a space and do a lively high jump with your whole body strongly stretched long or wide. Land softly and slowly with knees and ankles giving gently like springs.

Infant

LESSON 4 OF A 4-LESSON DEVELOPMENT

Theme *(a)* Planning and performing simple skills safely; *(b)* body shape awareness.
Concentrating on showing control in linking together the actions that have been planned, practised, improved and remembered during the preceding lessons.

FLOORWORK – 12 minutes

Legs

1 Run and jump high to show a clear body shape.

2 Be still after your 'squashy' landing, then look for a new space and off you go again.

3 In your sequence of running and jumping, can you show me:
   a a still start and finish
   b clear shapes in the air
   c a nicely balanced, soft landing, using your arms to steady you.

Body

1 Join the four balances, slowly and firmly, with no wobbling. Tiptoes... tilt to one side... lower to sitting... back to shoulders... and now back up to tiptoes standing.

2 Perform the routine once again, and keep a nice slow rhythm from start to finish. Stretch strongly the body parts not supporting you.

Arms

1 Show me your three or four slow travelling actions on hands and feet. Can you name the different actions?

2 I am looking at your body shapes and your directions.

3 Show me your best performance, to include:
   a stillness between the different travelling actions
   b different ways and directions to travel
   c clear shapes as you travel or pause in between.

APPARATUS WORK – 16 minutes

1 Travel, quietly, to visit all parts of the room space, touching only mats and floor. You can run and jump to land on a mat.

2 On 'Stop!', show me your best balance and strong body shape.

3 Stop! Next time, can you balance on different apparatus using a different body part? Stop!

4 Move freely from apparatus to apparatus. Find lots of spaces to show me your still balances. Can you include some long and wide; some tight curls; maybe an arch, or even a twisted shape? Keep going, travelling with neat, quiet actions.

5 Can you now, on apparatus, try some of those excellent travelling actions on hands and feet which I saw in the floorwork?

6 Can you show me how you can join up the following:
   a travelling on the floor on your feet, up to and away from apparatus
   b travelling on apparatus on hands and feet
   c holding a still balance in a firm shape on apparatus
   d jumping down from apparatus, with a soft landing.

FINAL FLOOR ACTIVITY – 2 minutes

Run and jump high with a whole body long or wide stretched shape.

Junior

LESSON 1 OF A 4-LESSON DEVELOPMENT

Theme Sequences and planning to link together a short series of actions on floor and apparatus.
Concentrating on *(a)* the neat, well-controlled actions being used; *(b)* how the body parts concerned are being used; *(c)* the body shapes used to enhance the appearance of the work.

FLOORWORK – 12 minutes

Legs

1 Using legs, plan to show me a triangle of actions, starting and finishing at the same place on the floor.

2 Can you include variety? Feet together, apart or passing each other? Walking, running, jumping, skipping, bouncing; big or small?

3 Show me clear, firm body shapes thoughout. No sagging!

Body

1 Stay in your floor space and show me a short sequence of two or three favourite balances, all neatly linked.

2 Can you include a variety of supporting body parts?

3 Can you stretch arms or legs, if they are not being used to support you, to make your work look neater?

Arms

1 Slowly, can you show me three different actions you can use, while travelling on feet and hands only?

2 Can you recognise and name the actions? For example, bunny jumps, cartwheels, crawling, hands, then feet, bouncing.

3 Which body parts are leading the actions?

4 Can you include more than one clear body shape?

APPARATUS WORK – 16 minutes

1 As you visit each set of apparatus, moving round, anti-clockwise, can you show me a simple pattern of travelling up to, on and off apparatus, quickly. Each finishing place becomes your starting place for the next apparatus.

2 Which actions are you using to travel up to and from the apparatus?

3 Which actions on to and from the apparatus allow a 'quick' response?

4 Can you expand your sequence at each place by including a balance, held still for three seconds, with a clear body shape?

5 Stay at one set of apparatus with four or five other pupils to plan, practise, improve and remember a sequence which includes:
a travelling on feet up to and from apparatus
b a still, firm balance with a clear body shape
c travelling on feet and hands along, across or around apparatus
d taking all your weight on your hands at some point.

FINAL FLOOR ACTIVITY – 2 minutes

Revise your triangle of leg activities with varied actions and good body shapes.

Junior

LESSON 2 OF A 4-LESSON DEVELOPMENT

Theme Sequences and planning to link together a short series of actions on floor and apparatus.
Concentrating on *(a)* revising the neat, well-controlled actions from lesson 1; *(b)* revising the clear body shapes to enhance the look of the work; *(c)* where the actions take place – own or whole room space; in what direction; and at what level, to add to the quality and variety of the actions.

FLOORWORK – 12 minutes

Legs

1 In your triangular sequence of three leg actions, can you include a change of direction, either within your travelling, or as you arrive at a point of your triangle?

2 Remember to emphasise your clear body shapes to make the work look more attractive, including your start and finish.

Body

1 In your sequence of two or three linked balances, can you show me your varied supporting body parts?

2 Can you balance at different levels, for example, high on tiptoes; medium on hands and feet; low, lying or arching?

3 Remember to stretch arms or legs if they are not used to support you. This strong shape looks neat and attractive.

Arms

1 Can you travel slowly on hands and feet and show me three actions which we might call 'different'?

2 The 'differences' are in what the hands and feet are doing – working together; alternately; high, medium or low.

3 Which body parts lead the actions – head, feet, one side?

APPARATUS WORK – 16 minutes

1 In your short sequence of travelling up to, on, and quickly away from the apparatus, can you include a direction change? For example, on facing forward, off facing sideways.

2 Remember not to linger on the apparatus. Move quickly off, please!

3 Expand your sequence by adding in a three-second balance with its clear shape, and by taking all your weight on your hands.

4 Vary your balances by using different body part supports on different parts of the apparatus – high, medium and low level.

5 Stay at your present group places with four of five others to practise, improve and remember your sequence which includes:
   a at least two ways to travel on the floor and mats
   b a still, firm balance with a clear body shape
   c travelling on feet and hands on apparatus
   d taking all your weight on your hands at some point, and
   e a change of direction to give your work more variety.

FINAL FLOOR ACTIVITY – 2 minutes

In your triangle of leg activities, with varied actions and good shapes, can you include one or more changes of direction?

Junior

LESSON 3 OF A 4-LESSON DEVELOPMENT

Theme Sequences and planning to link together a short series of actions on floor and apparatus.

Concentrating on *(a)* revising actions, good use of body parts and neat body shapes; *(b)* using space well to bring variety to the work; *(c)* the amount of effort and speed needed for a neat, controlled performance. How gentle or explosive? How fast or slow?

FLOORWORK – 12 minutes

Legs

1 Start and finish still and poised. Show me your triangle of three leg actions, including a change of direction.

2 Actions can use varied speed or effort. A small, slow, gentle action can contrast with a big, explosive, quicker one.

3 Feel a firm body tension with strong shapes throughout.

Body

1 In your sequence of two or three linked balances, show me your linking actions.

2 Feel the strong stretches in your arms and legs if they are not supporting your balances. This firmness looks very neat.

3 An interesting contrast can come from a quick, sudden spring up on to the feet from a slow move at a lower level.

Arms

1 In your slow travelling on feet and hands, are you including taking all your weight on your hands at one point, as in cartwheels, handstands or high bunny jumps?

2 Interesting variety can come from travelling sideways and backward, as well as forward.

3 Strong movements such as bouncing along on hands and feet, or cartwheels, contrast with the easier, low crawling actions.

APPARATUS WORK – 16 minutes

1 In your short sequence of travelling up to, on and off apparatus quickly, can you include interesting travelling on the floor as you did in the floorwork, either on your feet, or on hands and feet?

2 To contrast with the quick movement off the apparatus, can you show me a very slow travelling action, for example, a long, slow roll?

3 Travel on apparatus now, using hands and feet, and add a three-second still balance with a beautifully strong, firm body shape.

4 Stay at your starting apparatus to practise your sequence, starting and finishing on the floor and including:
   a interesting ways to travel up to and on to the apparatus, using your feet, and hands and feet, with direction changes
   b a balance, with a firm, clear body shape
   c taking all the weight on your hands at some point
   d changes of force and speed to make the work more interesting.

FINAL FLOOR ACTIVITY – 2 minutes

Include changes of direction, speed or force in your triangle of leg activity, travelling with varied actions and good body shapes.

Junior

LESSON 4 OF A 4-LESSON DEVELOPMENT

Theme Sequences and planning to link together a short series of actions on floor and apparatus.

Concentrating on (a) sequences that use and demonstrate all the skilfulness, knowledge and understanding that have been achieved during the several weeks of the lesson's development; (b) pupils working harder for longer, showing neat, accurate work which has variety, contrast and quality.

FLOORWORK – 12 minutes

Legs

In your triangle of varied travelling on feet, can you include:

a a still, poised start and finish

b a change of direction

c clear, firm body shapes throughout

d variety and contrast, using changes of effort or speed?

Body

In your sequence of linked balances on different body parts can you include:

a more than one level

b firm body shapes with non-supporting body parts stretched

c linking movements that might include a contrast of speed or effort?

Arms

In your repeating sequence of slow travelling actions on hands and feet, can you demonstrate:

a variety in your actions

b variety in directions used

c interesting combinations of feet and hand activity?

APPARATUS WORK – 16 minutes

In your groups of four of five, stay at your present set of apparatus to practise and improve your sequences to include:

a a neat start and finish on the floor away from the apparatus

b varied travelling actions on the floor and mats up to and away from the apparatus

c strong use of hands and feet travelling on the apparatus

d a three-second balance at some point

e taking all the weight strongly on hands, and

f changes of direction, speed and effort at one or more points, to give variety and interest to your performances, which we will be looking at.

FINAL FLOOR ACTIVITY – 2 minutes

In your final sequence, show me a triangle of impressive actions and superb body shapes, please.

Reception | Gymnastic programme

AUTUMN	SPRING	SUMMER
1 Stand still; look at and listen to the teacher; respond quietly to instructions, particularly request to 'Stop!'	**1** Respond wholeheartedly and quietly to simple tasks, working hard to improve.	**1** Respond readily, quietly and immediately to instructions.
2 Travel in a variety of ways, using feet – walking, running, jumping, skipping, galloping, hopping, bouncing, hopscotch.	**2** Practise, almost without stopping, until told to change to something else.	**2** Contribute unselfishly to the safe, quiet working environment.
3 Travel using hands and feet, slowly, with varied actions, shapes, directions and different parts leading.	**3** Use feet neatly, travelling in varied ways, sharing the limited space sensibly.	**3** Show pride and pleasure from achieving, having practised to improve.
4 Lift, carry, place apparatus safely and sensibly, working with others co-operatively.	**4** Travel slowly on hands and feet in varied ways, including 'bunny jumps' and cartwheels.	**4** Perform vigorously because 'It is good for our fitness.'
5 Be space aware, sharing floor and apparatus sensibly and unselfishly with others.	**5** Take weight safely on hands by keeping arms straight and head forward.	**5** Travel on hands and feet, with neat actions, good shapes and use of space.
6 Be shape aware, in stillness and travelling.	**6** Be aware of body parts used, and good body shapes, in travelling and stillness.	**6** Practise to improve the basic skills of running, jumping, rolling, climbing, hanging, inverting and balancing.
7 Enjoy linking a series of actions together, smoothly.	**7** Perform simple rolls, curled up small, and 'log rolls', sideways, with straight body.	**7** Take body weight safely on hands with straight arms and head forward, as in 'bunny jumps' and cartwheels.
8 Enjoy moving vigorously, believing 'These lessons are good for you, fun, exciting.'	**8** Plan responses to simple tasks. 'Can you show me … ?'	**8** Jump to land safely from low apparatus without jarring, by 'giving' in knees.
9 Demonstrate willingly when asked, to help observers, and to have own achievements recognised and explained.	**9** Practise landing from low apparatus without jarring, with a 'squashy give' in knees and ankles.	**9** Perform simple, side to side rolls, curled or 'log' rolls with stretched body.
10 Plan and perform simple skills safely.	**10** Lift, carry and place apparatus in co-operation with others.	**10** Be body shape aware – wide, long, curled, arched – still, balanced or travelling.
11 Observe simple actions being demonstrated and describe and learn from pleasing features.	**11** Co-operate and work sensibly with a partner.	**11** Understand 'Over, under, across, along, around' during apparatus work.
	12 Watch demonstrations and comment on good work seen. Copy some features.	**12** Take part in simple partner activities such as leading and following.
		13 Link a short series of simple actions such as walk, run, jump and land.
		14 When linking actions smoothly together, show a still start and finish position.
		15 Watch demonstrations with interest and be able to pick out and comment on features which are pleasing and worth copying.

Year 1 — Gymnastic programme

AUTUMN

1 Respond quietly and quickly to instructions, working continuously until stopped.
2 Co-operate unselfishly, sharing floor and apparatus space, for safe, free, unhindered movement.
3 Travel with neat, well planned and varied use of feet on floor and on apparatus.
4 Travel, using hands and feet, with varied actions and directions, on floor and on apparatus.
5 Be body shape aware, in balanced stillness, and in travelling, with good posture and body tension.
6 Roll smoothly from side to side; rock forward and back, and forward roll, when ready.
7 Lift, carry, place apparatus safely with others.
8 Produce almost non-stop, neat, quiet, thoughtful activity in floor and apparatus work.
9 Travel up to, on, along and from apparatus with a good repertoire of travelling and climbing actions.
10 Absorb shock when jumping and landing from apparatus.
11 Express pleasure in demonstrations by others, and pick out and praise pleasing features.

SPRING

1 Listen, then respond to instructions, thinking about own performance.
2 Be habitually active, striving to improve.
3 Show a caring attitude to self and others.
4 Understand and use safe methods of supporting all body weight on hands – straight arms, head looking forward.
5 Be space aware, performing in own space, and moving from space to good space.
6 Balance well on a variety of body parts, with good tension and firm shapes.
7 Jump and land safely, with no jarring, often with a direction change, from low apparatus.
8 Demonstrate an expanding repertoire of neat, well-controlled, varied movements.
9 Plan and perform sequences of simple, linked actions with still start and finish.
10 Work enthusiastically with increasing self-confidence.
11 Show pleasure from taking part in varied, vigorous enjoyable activity.
12 Describe what was observed using simple terms to identify the movements.

SUMMER

1 Respond immediately to each task set, showing a keen attitude and consideration of others sharing the space.
2 Experiment with varied actions, using opportunities given to repeat, practise and improve control and 'correctness'.
3 Practise, vary and enhance the basic actions of running, jumping, rolling, swinging, hanging, climbing, balancing and inverting.
4 Be body shape aware, able to show firm, clear, stretched, wide, curled, arched shapes in stillness, balance and movement.
5 Be body parts aware, understanding how parts receive, support and transfer body weight.
6 Be space aware, using different directions and levels, own and whole room space, for variety, contrast and greater interest.
7 Land well from apparatus with a 'squashy give' in knees and ankles.
8 Use swinging as an aid and impetus to movement.
9 Demonstrate varied ways to travel up to, on, along and from apparatus, emphasising 'No queues. Use floor as well as apparatus. Be found working, not waiting.'
10 Demonstrate sequences enthusiastically, working hard to perform well to help spectators.
11 Link together a short series of actions and practise to improve and remember them.
12 Work co-operatively with a partner, leading, following, working in unison.
13 Observe others' actions and answer questions on what was seen and liked, and what was worth learning or copying.

Year 2

Gymnastic programme

AUTUMN

1 Respond quickly to instructions, performing wholeheartedly, vigorously and safely.
2 Work, almost non-stop, trying to do neat, quiet performances.
3 Share floor and apparatus space unselfishly with others.
4 Pursue competence, originality and versatility by thoughtful, well-planned practising.
5 In travelling and flight, use vigorous, varied take-off and landing actions, using arms well for balance.
6 Support body weight on hands safely with straight arms, head forward, and just the right amount of effort in the push.
7 Include firm, still balances within sequences as contrast to continuous, vigorous action.
8 Be body shape aware to progress the work and improve its style.
9 Be body parts aware, 'feeling' how the parts are working.
10 Demonstrate increasing control and understanding by including direction and level changes.
11 Be reminded of correct, safe, way to lift, carry and place apparatus, working with others.
12 Link movements with control.
13 Observe a performance and comment on what was well done and worth copying.

SPRING

1 Show ability and desire to respond safely and quickly to tasks in varied ways.
2 Practise wholeheartedly and continuously, focusing on actions, body parts used, and good spacing.
3 Balance well on varied parts and show good, firm shapes.
4 Be effort and speed aware, feeling good body tension for a controlled performance.
5 Be body shape aware in stillness, balance, travelling.
6 Be keen to improve, working hard, alone, and with partner.
7 Co-operate with a partner to mirror, contrast, lead, follow.
8 Work, almost non-stop, with no queuing or impeding others.
9 Work hard to deserve praise and stamp work with own special style and personality.
10 Plan and perform sequences of actions linked neatly, quietly, with control and poise.
11 Show ability to approach, mount, travel on and leave apparatus without impeding others, and with interesting, versatile contrasts such as jumps, rolls, balances and inversion.
12 Observe performances with interest and suggest ways in which they might be improved.

SUMMER

1 Respond to set tasks with confidence and enthusiasm.
2 Manage the body in a well-controlled way, using the full range of movement in the joints and muscles concerned.
3 Show good space awareness – knowing how to slow down, speed up, pause to accommodate and not impede others sharing the space.
4 Use varied speeds and effort for more spectacular performances – explosive jumps, gentle rolls, firm balances, slow stretches and curls, strong climbs.
5 Co-operate with a partner, travelling together, copying each other, observing and commenting, and working in unison.
6 Show a well-practised expertise in lifting, carrying, placing apparatus, quickly, quietly and safely with others.
7 Feel that they have progressed and understand the nature of the progress, e.g. excellent jumps and landings; varied rolls; weight on hands with confidence; smooth rolls; and well-linked sequences.
8 Approach, mount, travel on and dismount from apparatus, responding to set tasks with confidence and enthusiasm.
9 Observe demonstrations and comment on actions and any features worth copying or learning from.
10 Recognise the effects of physical activity on bodies – deep breathing, faster pulse rate, feeling hot, becoming exhausted.

Year 3

Gymnastic programme

AUTUMN

1 Behave properly and dress sensibly.
2 Work quietly and almost non-stop.
3 Respond immediately to instruction.
4 Work hard to improve.
5 Share space sensibly and unselfishly, concerned for own and others' safety.
6 Lift, carry and place apparatus sensibly.
7 Move neatly with good control.
8 Learn safe practice skills such as 'squashy' landings; keeping arms straight with head looking forward when inverted on hands; putting thumbs under bars of climbing frames for a safe, strong grip.
9 Travel slowly on hands and feet, showing clear, thoughtful actions, on floor and on apparatus.
10 Showing good control in running, jumping, landing, able to adapt to the space available and to others.
11 Show variety in running, jumping, landing, aware of feet, leg and arm actions at take-off, in flight and on balanced landings.
12 Show body parts awareness in jumps, landing, climbing and balancing.
13 Understand body shapes – long, wide, curled, arched, twisted.
14 Link a series of simple actions and be able and keen to repeat it.
15 Observe others' actions and answer questions on what was seen.

SPRING

1 Practise, refine and adapt basic activities of jumping, rolling, climbing, swinging, balancing, and taking weight on hands.
2 Link together short series of actions on floor and apparatus, with poised beginnings, middles and ends.
3 Respond imaginatively to challenges – 'Can you ... ?'
4 Balance on varied supporting body parts at different levels.
5 Demonstrate shape awareness by interesting use in sequences.
6 Make appropriate decisions quickly in planning thoughtful responses.
7 Work vigorously, inspiring deep breathing and perspiration.
8 Co-operate with a partner to create own sequences.
9 Try hard to develop performance.
10 Understand the contribution of shape to quality and variety and maintain good posture always.
11 Be instantly adaptable in sharing space with and being considerate towards others.
12 Demonstrate understanding through physical responses.
13 Demonstrate enthusiastically and comment readily on good features of others' performances.

SUMMER

1 Display greater control and neatness in basic actions.
2 Respond to a variety of tasks by planning, refining and adapting performance.
3 Link movements in a logical sequence that can be repeated and enhanced with contrasts of shape, speed and good use of space.
4 Apply the right amount of effort in jumps, rolls and balances for efficient performance.
5 Learn simple, traditional gymnastic skills such as rolls, balances and vaults.
6 Work co-operatively with a partner, learning sequences not possible alone.
7 Recognise the value of contrasts in making work look more interesting.
8 Sustain energetic activity for longer periods.
9 Observe others performing and suggest ways in which they might improve.
10 Give an impression of whole-hearted, enthusiastic participation at all times.

Year 4 — Gymnastic programme

AUTUMN	SPRING	SUMMER
1 Co-operate sensibly to provide a safe, quiet working environment.	1 Consolidate particular skills by practice and repetition.	1 Use swinging as an aid to movement in floor and apparatus work.
2 Respond readily and quickly to instructions.	2 Develop body shape awareness in held and moving positions.	2 Practise rolls, forward, back, side to side, aided by impetus of the swing.
3 Respond wholeheartedly and with vigour to challenges.	3 Include clear shapes within sequences to enhance them and provide variety and contrast.	3 Swing up to handstand, choosing arm or leg swing as own preference.
4 Share space unselfishly to enable self and others to work properly and safely.	4 Learn safe, traditional skills – rolls, cartwheels, vaults and balances.	4 Plan apparatus sequences to start and finish on the floor, away from apparatus.
5 Plan ahead to visualise the intended outcome.	5 Revise correct, safe grips and handholds on apparatus, and hands, arms and head position when inverted on hands.	5 Include swings, rolls and taking weight on hands within apparatus sequences.
6 Plan to include varied actions performed neatly and quietly.	6 Improve quality and variety with space features such as different directions, levels and own and general space.	6 Apply speed and effort factors to make work look more controlled, varied, demanding, interesting.
7 Develop a tradition of continuous work, always aware of need to share space with others.	7 With still start and finish, practise, adapt, improve and be able to repeat longer, more complex sequences.	7 Work harder for longer with better control.
8 Include contrasts of speed, shape, effort and use of space to enhance performances.	8 Extend balance possibilities on floor and apparatus, always aware of clear shapes and different levels.	8 Balance, feeling contrast between one, firm, held balance and the more relaxed transfer to the next.
9 Practise, repeat, adapt and try to improve.	9 Recognise and describe good features of a demonstration.	9 Apply strong effort to develop strength and suppleness, and to exercise the heart and the lungs.
10 Use the full range of movement possible in the joints concerned.	10 Give the impression of habitually sustaining and enjoying energetic activity.	10 Make quick decisions, e.g. in matching a partner.
11 Practise different ways to do basic actions – travel, jump, roll, swing, climb, balance and take weight on hands.		11 Remember and repeat work exactly to enable partner to learn it.
12 Feel and understand how body parts work to support, receive and transfer body weight.		12 Be aware of features to watch in a partner's demonstration – actions; body parts involved; shapes; directions; speed and effort.
13 Comment generously on the main features of a performance observed, and what was liked.		13 Encourage demonstrators with favourable, encouraging comments.

85

Year 5 — Gymnastic programme

AUTUMN

1 Participate and co-operate unselfishly. Aim to improve and be told you have improved.
2 In longer, more skilful sequences, start and finish, still, and link movements neatly to maintain flow.
3 Modify initial attempts to achieve an intended result.
4 Introduce direction changes for variety and safety.
5 In balances, use varied parts for support, often linking the balances by rolls.
6 Revise safe grips on bars, boxes, benches, ropes and safe hand and arm positions while inverted on hands.
7 Practise, almost non-stop, always aware of others. 'Be found working, not waiting.'
8 Maintain good posture; be physically active, using joints to their full range.
9 Help self by making simple comments on own and others' performances.
10 Plan, practise, improve, remember, and be able to repeat the longer sequences.

SPRING

1 Practise enthusiastically to improve and consolidate skills.
2 Experience different shapes in held positions, while travelling, and in flight.
3 Improve the appearance of the work with 'firm', clear shapes.
4 Work harder for longer in almost non-stop action, in creating own planned sequences.
5 Learn safe ways to land, grip, travel, balance, hang, swing.
6 Perform effectively in activities needing quick decision-making.
7 Improve quality and variety through varied shapes, levels, direction and speed.
8 Make more adventurous use of own personal and whole room, shared space, directions and levels.
9 Sustain energetic activity by wholehearted, vigorous activity.
10 Learn or improve simple, traditional gymnastic skills including rolls, balances, rope climbs, vaults, hand balances.
11 Comment on a performance and suggest ways to improve it.

SUMMER

1 Be able to repeat movements learned previously.
2 Plan appropriate use of space to respond to challenges to travel on floor and apparatus.
3 Make quick decisions during non-stop travelling, finding space by looking ahead.
4 Explore different means of rolling, taking weight on hands, balancing, running and jumping.
5 Refine and repeat longer sequences, emphasising changes of speed, effort, shape, direction or level to enhance the appearance of the work.
6 Plan to demonstrate neat, quiet and accurate performances; to work thoughtfully; and then plan again for higher standards.
7 Work co-operatively with a partner, adapting favourite movement patterns to accommodate another.
8 Demonstrate understanding through the ability to observe, copy and repeat partner's demonstrations.
9 Be aware of and include contrasting actions for greater quality, variety and enhanced appearance.
10 Make a positive contribution within group activity.
11 Analyse two performances and indicate differences in content, quality and effectiveness.

Year 6 — Gymnastic programme

AUTUMN	SPRING	SUMMER
1 Re-establish good traditions for optimum level of enjoyment, safety and achievement – quick responses to instructions; good sharing of floor and apparatus; working hard to improve.	1 Adopt good posture always and use body safely and sensibly in lifting and carrying, jumping and landing, rolling and upending.	1 Recognise the importance of, and value an active lifestyle. 'What you don't use, you lose.'
2 Work vigorously to develop strength and suppleness, and to exercise heart and lungs.	2 Respond imaginatively to challenges, doing one's best to produce quiet, neat, controlled work with enthusiasm.	2 Understand the value of, and be able to sustain, vigorous physical activity.
3 Demonstrate originality and versatility in neat, well-controlled work.	3 Understand the value of, and demonstrate, sustained activity.	3 Revise and improve traditional skills; mat agilities; circles and climbs on a rope; balances on inverted benches; circling on bars; head and handstands.
4 Explore different means of rolling, balancing, jumping.	4 Work and practise hard, with determination until a task is mastered.	4 Make appropriate decisions quickly in planning responses.
5 Improve skills of rope climbing; travelling on hands and feet; rolling, balancing.	5 Emphasise changes of shape with a constant concern for good looking, poised movements.	5 Plan longer sequences, able to envisage the finished product, and showing aesthetic qualities, including contrast, variety and repetition.
6 Enhance sequences by including contrasts of shape, speed, effort, direction or level.	6 Be space aware, expressed in changes of direction and level, and varied use of own and the general shared space.	6 Observe, copy, contrast or match a partner's movements, developing one's powers of observation and an awareness of the elements of movement.
7 Plan and perform, knowing, for example, start and finish places; places to jump, to roll and to balance.	7 Demonstrate good use of effort to achieve a well-controlled performance.	7 Plan appropriate solutions, sometimes imaginatively, to the various challenges encountered.
8 Improve body parts awareness, understanding how hands, feet and larger parts carry, support, propel, grip and act generally.	8 Display understanding, generally, by its effect on planning.	8 Improve, refine and repeat a series of movements performed previously, with increasing control and accuracy.
9 Plan, practise, improve and remember more complex sequences.	9 Refine and adapt performance when working with a partner.	9 Make judgements about own and others' performance, and use this information to improve the accuracy, quality and variety of performance.
10 Appraise a sequence of movement using relevant terminology.	10 Perform with a sense of commitment.	
	11 Recognise when a sequence is appropriate to the aims of the performer.	

Dance

The focus is on the body, developing control, co-ordination and versatility to become a more poised and graceful mover. Vigorous actions and movements also develop strength and suppleness.

The skills of dance include travelling, jumping, turning, rolling, rising, falling, opening, closing, gesture, balance and stillness. The lesson starts with simple, warming-up activities to encourage lively and responsive participation and a focused beginning. The middle section of the lesson develops the actions, movements or ideas which are the main theme. For the final, most important part of the lesson, pupils select and use the ideas for their created dance.

Dance is creative and the aim, first and foremost, is to make and present something original as the outcome of a series of lessons. The created dance will be unique to the individual, pair or group who devise it.

Feelings and ideas are expressed through body movement, as in angry stamping of feet; joyful gesturing of arms – 'Goal!'; or a self-confident swaggering of shoulders. Dance is an extra and universal means of communicating, using our body. It is hoped, also, that pupils will express pride in their achievements and that 'dance is fun!'

The artistic and aesthetic nature of dance is developed by understanding and applying the movement elements that enhance the quality of a performance. Variety and contrast in the use of body action, shape, direction, level, speed and body tension, make a dance more interesting, attractive and exciting, and potentially a moving experience for both performer and spectator.

Dance is sociable, friendly and co-operative. Achievement is often shared with a partner or a group, leading to a sense of fellowship and togetherness with others who helped create 'our dance'.

It has been said that 'Dance is all about making, remembering and repeating patterns.' Whether we are performing a created dance or an existing folk dance, there will be a still start and finish and an arrangement of repeated parts within.

The number, length and complexity of the repeating parts will depend on the age and experience of the class. A simple, two-part, skipping and bouncing; skipping and bouncing, individual repeating pattern with infants can become a longer stepping, skipping, clapping and gesture; stepping, skipping, clapping and gesture, four-part, repeating pattern with juniors in lines of four.

STIMULI FOR DANCE

A stimulus is a starting point, used to capture the interest of the class, provide a focus for their attention, and inspire in them a desire for movement. A dance stimulus is something you:

- enjoy doing, such as natural actions. Pupils will immediately start to walk, run, jump, skip, hop, bounce or gallop, whether accompanied by music or percussion, following the teacher/leader or responding to the teacher calling out the actions

- can see. Objects like a leaf, branch, balloon, ball, bubbles, puppets, piece of material, elastic or rag doll can all be made to move and suggest movement ideas to children

- can hear. Sounds that can stimulate movement include:
  a medium to quick, rhythmic tempo music, including folk dance
  b percussion instruments – tambourine, drum, cymbal, clappers

c body contact sounds – clapping hands, stamping feet, tapping feet, clicking fingers, slapping body

d rhythmically chanting words or phrases – names, numbers, place names, items of food

e action songs, chanted rhymes and nursery rhymes

- have seen on a visit, on television or in a photograph. Of particular interest to infant school pupils are:

  a zoo animals – elephants, penguins, dolphins, seals, monkeys

  b circus performers – clowns, jugglers, trapeze artists, acrobats

  c seaside play – swimming, paddling, floating, rowing, making sandcastles, and movements of the waves

  d children's playground activities – climbing, swinging, throwing and catching, skipping

- experience seasonally – spring and growth, summer holidays and fairgrounds, autumn and harvest, winter snow and frost, Guy Fawkes, fireworks, halloween, Diwali, Christmas toys, circus and pantomime, Easter eggs

- are doing in class that lends itself to a dance – air and flight, magnetism, animals and birds, climate, pond life, water, rivers and waterfalls, machines, life cycles, space travel, poems, stories and movement, expressive topics such as relationships or conflict

- consider 'newsworthy' or of human interest – charity appeals, road safety, Olympic Games, extremes of weather, newly arrived pupil, hobbies, family, friendship.

Whatever the stimulating starting point, the teacher must convert it into the language of action. Children cannot 'be' leaves, but they can 'Travel on tiptoes with light, floating movements, tilting and turning, slowly.' They cannot 'be' machines, but they can 'Try pushing down actions, like corks into bottles, on the spot, turning or moving along, as on an assembly line.' They cannot 'be' clowns, but they can 'Do a funny walk on heels, spin round with one leg high, fall down slowly, bounce up, and repeat.'

TEACHING DANCE

Dance might appear to be the easiest subject to teach because there are no elusive and unpredictable implements hampering a lesson's flow as in Games, and there is no large apparatus to lift, carry, place and use safely and sensibly, as in Gymnastic Activities.

In fact, Dance is the hardest subject to teach because a Dance lesson needs the constant involvement of the teacher. A popular game can keep a class busy for long periods with little teacher input, while apparatus work in Gymnastic Activities inspires so many exciting, challenging actions that pupils can be kept busy, even if the teacher has little to say.

This 'ongoing potential' for minimum teacher involvement does not apply to dance. A dance, once completed and presented, does not have the prolonged 'shelf life' of a game or apparatus work. Teacher and class have to move on, together, to their next, probably completely different dance.

We do not always need a story or a big theme as a starting point. Action words called out by the teacher, or seen on a card, can almost instantly get the class working because the task is specific. The creative development should be equally clear, for example, 'Make a short sequence using skip, stretch and turn in the order you choose.'

Everyone can use their imagination but they need to be clear about what they are being asked to do and when to do it, when challenged to create more expressive sequences and patterns; guidance must be specific. The teacher's difficult task is to remove all vagueness and give the class an easily visualised, clearly understood image so that they know what they are doing.

If pupils are set the vague tasks – 'Find ways...', 'Make shapes...', or 'Explore levels...', they will not understand why they are finding, making or exploring, because there is no obvious end to it. Such a task is not specific enough and does not conjure up an easily visualised image.

Doing 'Creeping and crawling' is much more purposeful if we are moving like a burglar about to enter a house. Balancing like a tight rope walker is much more interesting than being told to 'Travel slowly along a straight line.' Within the theme 'Nature', 'Explore being a butterfly' is far too loose and vague. Instead, we can look at the life cycle of the butterfly:

a egg – all curled up as individuals

b wiggling up and down of caterpillar

c into fluttering, flying butterfly, which can be represented by one or four dancers together, and then

d it dies.

The dance has been given form and structure. Teacher and class have a clear picture in their heads; they know what to do, when to do it, and they know where the dance is going.

PATTERNS WITHIN DANCE

The dictionary defines 'pattern' as 'an arrangement of repeated parts'. Whether we are performing a dance created by the teacher and the class, or an already created folk dance, the dance will have a still starting and finishing position and an arrangement of repeated parts within. Such repetition helps the dancers to remember the dance and repeatedly practise its parts to improve.

A 'Bubbles' dance with infants might include a pattern of 'Floating... gliding... sinking... and... burst!' which will be repeated at each time of performing, helped by the teacher's commentary and reminders.

A 'Machines' dance with juniors can have a more complex and demanding pattern of (a) individual activity; (b) moving to partner activity; (c) combining in lines of four activity; (d) a whole class unit of factory or assembly line activity. Within each of these four parts of the overall pattern, there will be patterns to practise, repeat and remember.

A good pattern for a longer dance is (a) teacher directed start; (b) pupil created middle; and (c) teacher directed finish. For example, the teacher can direct the start of the 'Circus' dance with the parade coming into town, the assembling of the big top, and two, whole class work actions such as trapeze artists and tight rope walkers – always with a repeating pattern so they can be remembered. In their own spaces, the several groups of four pupils then decide their own choice of work action, and

plan their own repeating pattern to identify it (e.g. pairs of trapeze artists swing towards each other, then back, then forward and back, then forward and change places). The teacher then directs the end of the dance, lowering the big top and parading out of town.

A typical 32-bar English or Scottish country dance will have a four-part repeating pattern which makes the dance easy to repeat, improve and remember. For example, a simple, partners circle dance:

Bars 1–8 All skip to centre and back;

Bars 9–16 Chasse sideways to centre and back;

Bars 17–24 Promenade, anti-clockwise;

Bars 25–32 Turn partners, four counts to right and four to left;
Keep repeating.

For the teacher, a pattern for developing a dance might be:

a a stimulating starting point. 'In our 'Toy Shop' dance there will be penguins for us to think about.'

b convert the stimulus into the language of action. 'Let me see you walking tall, but leaning from side to side as you go. With your flippers down at your sides, can you make little swimming movements?'

c encourage pupils to arrange their actions into a repeating pattern. 'Can you waddle, waddle, waddle; swim, swim, swim? Waddle, waddle, waddle; swim, swim, swim.'

SIMPLE IDEAS FOR WARMING-UP ACTIVITIES

The warming-up, introductory activity is important because it can create the right co-operative, industrious and thoughtful start to the lesson. A successful warm-up establishes good habits of attentive, quiet, wholehearted working and spacing. It encourages the class to move with good poise and body tension and it helps them think about and feel their bodies moving rhythmically. It should also be enjoyable, put the class in the mood for dance and make them relax and move freely after being seated in the classroom.

Many warming-up activities have the potential to be developed as the middle section of the lesson and, eventually, the created dance climax of the lesson. This happens most easily with travelling actions which can develop, for example, into a 'Follow My Leader', 'Clever Feet', 'Space Travel' or 'Going and Stopping' dance.

1 Eight steps on the spot alternate with eight travelling steps. 'Step on the spot, 3, 4, 5, 6, ready to go; travel, travel, 3, 4, 5, 6, start again.'

2 Four steps on the spot, arms at sides; four steps turning with hand claps to face a good space; four steps, travelling with arm swings; four steps travelling with high hand claps. 'Steps on the spot, 3, 4; turn and clap, 3, 4; travel, travel, good arm swing; travel, travel, clap hands high; start again, steps on the spot.'

3 Walk for seven counts, jump to face a new direction on '8'; skip for seven counts, jump to face a new direction on '8'. 'Walk forward, 3, 4, 5, 6, jump and turn; skip, skip, 3, 4, 5, 6, jump and turn.'

4 Skip for six counts, make friendly hand contact with someone near on '7' and '8', saying 'Hello! Hello!' 'Skip, 2, 3, 4, 5, 6, meet and speak. Skip quietly, 3, 4, 5, 6, smile and speak.'

5 a Little bounces on the spot for eight.
b March with good arm swings for eight.
c Clap hands and skip on the spot for eight.

d Walk for six counts, say 'Hello! Hello!' to someone near on '7, 8'. 'Bounce, bounce, nice and soft, 5, 6, 7, 8; march, march, swing the arms, 5, 6, 7, 8; clap and skip, clap and skip, 5, 6, 7, 8; walk, walk, 3, 4, 5, 6, 'Hello! Hello!'

6 a Travel freely, in and out of one another. When the drum sounds twice, join with a partner to travel together.
b When the drum sounds once, separate and dance by yourself.
c When drum sounds twice, join with a different partner. Repeat **b** and **c**.

7 Circle formation.
a All skip into centre for four, stay and clap hands for four, stepping on the spot.
b All turn and do four chasse steps out sideways, back to places in circle.
c In own starting places, do a favourite action.

Keep repeating.

8 Circle formation. As **7**, it fits well to any 32-bar folk dance music and keeps repeating its 4 × 8 pattern.
a All walk in to the centre for four counts and clap, walk back to circle places for four.
b All skip in to the centre for four counts and clap, skip back to circle places for four.
c All bounce, feet together, for four counts, into the centre and clap, bounce back out, feet apart, for four.
d On the spot, in the circle, all skip, turning and rolling forearms round each other, as in 'Hornpipe', for eight counts.

9 Responding to a sound. 'Show me your favourite ways of travelling to all parts of the room, listening to the drum beat. When the drum stops – suddenly sometimes – quickly show me a body shape that is still and balanced. (Drum beats for different lengths of time and the silences in between are varied in their length.)

10 Isolating body parts for a partner to mirror. 'Decide who is leading and who is copying exactly. Leader, move one body part at a time, very slowly. It is a good idea to work downwards from the head to your feet and ankles.'

11 Using eyes to find empty spaces. 'Move to an empty space near you and make a tiny body shape. Go! Now move to a new space and fill it with a huge body shape. Go! Keep moving, space to space, showing me your tiny and your huge body shapes.'

12 Making shapes in a circle. 'Sit where I can see you. As you sit there, your body, arms, legs and head are all making a shape. Look at other people's shape. Feel and remember your own shape. When Emma counts to "Three!" we all have to change to a new body shape, still sitting. Emma, count please.'

'Well done. You have all changed shape. Leroy, count, and this time we change to a lying or kneeling shape. Count please, Leroy.'

'Well done, again. Now, with Susan counting, please show me a strange, jagged or twisted shape – very difficult – but you are all working brilliantly today. Please count, Susan.'

13 Partners travelling to lively country dance music. 'With your partner, travel freely. You can be joined with one or both hands, or leading and following, or side by side but not joined.'

14 A song. Instant circle dance for infants as they join in with the teacher's words, said slowly, and the actions:

'Two little hands go clap, clap, clap,
Two little feet go tap, tap, tap,
Two little hands go bump, bump, bump,
Two little feet go jump, jump, jump,
One little body turns around,
One little child sits quietly down.'

THE CREATIVE DANCE LESSON PLAN

1 **Warming-up activities** aim to inspire an enjoyable, lively start to the lesson and put the class in the mood for dance. The activities need to be simple enough to get the whole class working, almost immediately, often by following the teacher who calls out and demonstrates the activities, which do not need to relate to the theme or main emphasis of the lesson.

Some form of travelling, using the feet, is the usual warming-up activity, with a specific way of moving being asked for. It might be to demonstrate better use of space, greater variety, greater control, good poise and body tension, or simply an enthusiastic use of all the body parts to warm up.

2 **Teaching and developing the movement skills and patterns** to be used in the new dance. Teaching methods include challenging, questioning, use of good demonstrations, and direct teaching.

a 'Kneel down and curl to your smallest shape. Show me how you can start to grow, very slowly. Are you starting with your back, head, shoulders, elbows or arms? Show me clearly how you rise to a full, wide stretch position.'

b 'If gesturing is like speaking with your body's movements, how might your body gesture to say "I am angry"?' Stamp feet, clench fists, punch the air, jump up and down heavily?

c 'How are the bubbles (made by teacher and pupils) moving? Where are they going?' Floating gently, gliding smoothly, soaring from low to higher, sinking slowly?

3 **Create and perform the dance.**

a 'Slowly, start to grow and show me which parts are leading as you rise to your full, wide flower shape in our "Spring" dance. You might even twist your flower shape to look at the sun.'

b 'Find a partner for our "Gestures" dance and decide who is asking a favour by gesturing with body actions to say "Please! I'm desperate! I need it! I must have it!". The other partner's body actions are saying "Never! You must be joking! Go away!" When we look at demonstrations, later, we will decide who the most expressive winners are.'

c 'For our "Bubbles" dance, I will say the four actions that we have practised – floating, gliding, soaring, sinking – slowly, and you will show me how you have planned to dance them.'

Depending on its complexity, a dance will be repeated two to four times to allow sufficient time for repetition, practice and improvement to take place, and a satisfactory performance to be achieved and presented.

Reception
Lesson 1 · 25 minutes

Theme Travelling with neat footwork and varied directions as pupils walk, run, jump, skip, bounce, gallop, slide.

WARM-UP ACTIVITIES – 4 minutes

1 All stand in a big circle, ready to do travelling actions. Let's sing the words and do the actions.

'This is the way we walk to school, walk to school, walk to school,
This is the way we walk to school on a cold and frosty morning.
This is the way we skip in the hall, skip in the hall, skip in the hall,

This is the way we skip in the hall on a cold and frosty morning.
This is the way we run outside, run outside, run outside,
This is the way we run outside, on a cold and frosty morning.'

2 That was very good. Let's do it again. Pretend it is a cold and frosty morning and we need to do lively actions to keep warm.

MOVEMENT SKILLS TRAINING – 15 minutes

1 Let us follow the drum as it tells us what actions to do.

2 It says 'March like a soldier and swing your arms. Now tiptoe, walking with tiny steps. Now skip and skip and swing your arms. Feet together, bounce along, 1, 2, 3, 4. Slide your feet along the floor. Gallop and gallop, 3, 4, lifting your feet high off the floor. Run, run, run and jump! Run, run, run and jump!'

3 Well done. That was good fun, following the drum leader. Let's practise again and try to space apart better. Pretend you each have a drum leader, looking for and taking you to good spaces where you won't bump into anyone.

4 Ready? Keep in time with the drum. Marching... tiptoe steps... skips... bounces... gallops... run and jump, run and jump and stop! Show me your still, finishing shape.

DANCE • FOLLOW THE DRUM – 6 minutes

1 For our dance, let's do 'Follow The Drum'. The drum will beat at different speeds with pauses in between the actions for you to show a strong shape, ready for the next action.

2 With the drum, ready... begin! (Short 10–12 second beat, then the one loud beat which says 'Stop!' The still, held shape period before the next and different drum beat is about four seconds, long enough for an infant to hold.)

3 That was excellent. All sit down, listen to the drum and tell me what actions you think it is suggesting. (Hopefully, they will say 'Galloping... walking... skipping.... sliding... bouncing', and be told 'Yes, well done'.)

4 Stand up and show me your still starting position and shape. This time I will not be telling you the different actions. Start and stop with the drum and make the actions fit the sound each time.

Reception

Lesson 2 30 minutes

Theme Christmas

WARM-UP ACTIVITIES – 4 minutes

1 Skip in your own space. Skip, skip, 3, 4, 5, 6, 7 and stop!

2 Clap hands in different spaces, high, low, in front or to side. Clap, clap, 3, 4, clap, clap, 7 and 8. (Repeat skips and claps.)

3 Skip, travelling for 6 counts. On 7 and 8, face a partner to do gentle hand claps. Skip and travel, 3, 4, 5, 6, face a partner.

4 Clap hands with your partner for 8 counts. Use one or both hands. Clap, clap, 3, 4, gently clap, skip again (and clap on 7, 8).

5 Brilliant! For the last four claps, you may say 'Happy Christmas when it comes!' Go! Skip, skip, 3, 4, 5, 6, find a partner; clap, clap, 3, 4, Happy Christmas, when it comes! Skip, skip... (repetitions).

MOVEMENT SKILLS TRAINING – 14 minutes

1 March, swinging arms proudly, to the tambourine beat. When it shakes, do a marching turn on the spot, and then off again.

2 March, march, 3, 4, swing your arms, now we turn; turn, turn, 3, 4, on the spot, then travel again. (Several repetitions for practice.)

3 Stand with body parts all loose and saggy, not like the firm body as we marched. Let head, shoulders and arms droop down in front of you. You feel as if you have no bones.

4 Now be slowly lifted up by an invisible string tied to your hands. Reach hands right up above head. Oh! Someone has cut the string and you collapse again. (Repeat up and drop.)

5 Lean forward at the waist, with straight arms out sideways, like wings. Show me how you can fly, glide, hover and zoom to different spaces. Remember to tilt your body to one side as you turn.

6 Lean forward from your waist with one arm hanging forward and one arm hanging behind. Show me your slow, heavy elephant way of walking, with your trunk and your tail.

DANCE • TOY FACTORY – 12 minutes

1 In our 'Toy Factory' dance, the toy maker has had a long and tiring day, getting all the toys ready for Christmas. He locks up and goes home. The toys, like young children, all love to move and play.

2 Let's all move like the toy soldier on the spot, marching, arms and legs swinging proudly, then turning on the spot.

3 Now, rag dolls, hang limp and loose until you feel the string pulling you up straight, then dropping you again.

4 Aeroplanes, fly, rising and lowering; hover, sometimes on the spot; lean in to your turns at the corners; fly round one another.

5 Huge elephants, with heavy steps, reach forward with your trunk and swish your tail behind.

6 Sit down and decide which toy you want to be – soldier, rag doll, aeroplane or elephant. Each group will dance by itself, then we can all work together until the toy maker comes back in the morning.

7 Get ready, soldiers. Go!... Rag dolls... Aeroplanes... Elephants... Now everyone, filling the toy factory with exciting action.

8 Rattle, rattle at the door. Back to places, still once more.

Year 1

Lesson 1 25 minutes

Theme Vocal sounds as movement accompaniment and inspiration

WARM-UP ACTIVITIES – 5 minutes

1 Listen to the rhythm of the lively music as you walk, run, skip, bounce, hop, gallop or run and jump. When I sound the tambourine twice, find a partner and dance together. You can be joined or separate. Go!

2 When the tambourine sounds once, separate and dance by yourself.

3 When the tambourine sounds twice, find a partner, different to the one you had before, and dance together.

MOVEMENT SKILLS TRAINING – 10 minutes

1 1 am going to sing out some of the actions we have done in our dance lessons. Listen carefully and try to keep going with my words. Some of the words might be stretched out and others might be shortened. Are you ready?

2 W-a-l-k; be still; f-l-o-p; stretch; s-k-i-p; stamp; t-u-r-n; clap; c-u-r-l; balance. Well done. You kept with me splendidly.

3 We can also move to other words that aren't movement words. Try moving to 'Tick tock'

just where you are. Say it and do it for me. Tick tock, small move, tick tock, light and quick.

4 Show me how you can travel to a wind blowing sound – whoosh!

5 Can you be brilliant and invent a sound or two sounds I have never heard before, and show me how you can move to them? Join the sounds and the movements exactly together.

6 Make your movements and shapes neat and let me hear your invented sounds loud and clear.

DANCE • VOICE SOUNDS – 10 minutes

1 Can you think of some holiday action words to use to accompany a short dance, if we stretch out or shorten parts of the word? Swimming... paddling... playing... painting... shopping... flying.

2 Can anyone tell me a place where you might be going that is an interesting word to dance to? Florida... Majorca... Scotland.

3 Decide your action word or place name, and then practise your short dance, saying the word and trying to include stillness, travelling, a jump, and maybe a turn or a rise and fall.

4 Take a deep breath before you start so that you can make one or more parts of the word s-t-r-e-t-ch out and be interesting to listen to and watch. You can also suddenly speed up a part of the word as a surprise.

5 Finish your little dance beautifully still, with a shape that makes me want to look at you.

6 Well done everyone. I saw lots of good action and I heard lots of interesting voice sounds. Let's have each half of the class in turn watching and commenting on the other half.

7 When you are watching, look out for and tell me about good actions, good shapes, and excellent use of the voice when saying the movement word.

Year 1

Theme Body parts awareness

WARM-UP ACTIVITIES – 5 minutes

1 Let's move round, singing and doing these actions together.

'If you're happy and you know it, clap your hands,

If you're happy and you know it, clap your hands,

If you're happy and you know it, and you really want to show it,

If you're happy and you know it, clap your hands.

If you're happy and you know it, stamp your feet,

… bend your knees… wave your arms… shake all over.'

MOVEMENT SKILLS TRAINING – 12 minutes

1 Show me some happy travelling actions to visit all parts of the room.

2 Stop and look at these four happy travellers and their skipping, galloping, bouncing, running and jumping.

3 Find a partner for 'Follow My Leader', with each of you showing the other your happy travelling actions. Watch your partner's feet, legs and whole body to try to copy and follow. Change leader when I call 'Change!' Off you go.

4 Now stand, facing your partner. Show me these friendly hand actions. Wave one hand, wave other hand; clap both hands gently, 1, 2, 3, 4, starting high and coming down, down, down to just in front of you both. Wave, wave; clap, clap, clap, clap.

5 Let's keep a nice, slow rhythm this time – wave, wave; clap, 2, 3, 4; high wave, high wave; high claps, both hands, lower and lower. Friendly wave and wave; friendly claps, claps, claps, stop!

DANCE • FOLLOW MY LEADER – 8 minutes

1 Partners, stand ready, one behind the other. When I call 'Travel!' the leader will show his or her lively, happy travelling for the partner to copy. When I call 'Stop!' partners face each other.

2 Try not to lose your partner by rushing ahead too far. Show your partner neat actions in your feet and legs, to see and copy. Stand ready now for the other one to lead when I call 'Travel!'

3 Travel! Look for spaces, leaders, please, and keep repeating your one or two actions.

4 Stop! Face each other and show me your waves and your handclaps at a nice slow speed – wave, wave; clap, clap, clap and stop!

5 Well done, new leaders and followers. In our next practice, you will decide when to change from travelling to waving and clapping, and when to start travelling again. All ready? Begin.

Year 2

Lesson 1 30 minutes

Theme Clowns
Music *TV Sport* by Central Band of the RAF

WARM-UP ACTIVITIES – 5 minutes

1 Let's try an '8:4:2' warm-up and see if you can keep with me. Eight skips forward... go! Skip, 2, 3, 4, 5, 6, 7, stop!

2 Good. You all started and stopped with me. Now an easy 4 steps backwards... go! Step, 2, 3 and stop!

3 We've gone forward. We've gone backward. What direction do you think we will go next?

Yes, sideways, with 2 chasse steps. Do it slowly with me. Step to side; close feet together; step to side; close feet together. Now, a little bit quicker. Side-step, close; side-step, close. Well done. Now, let's try the whole of our '8:4:2'. Skip forward, 3, 4, 5, 6, 7, 8; step backward, 3, 4; side-step, close; side-step, close. Excellent. Again ... go!

MOVEMENT SKILLS TRAINING – 15 minutes

1 Can you show me a funny clown walk? Can you turn your toes in a long way, swing your arms across your chest, and swing your shoulders up and down a long way?

2 You might try your funny walk going backward and sideways as well as forward. Four each way is a good pattern.

3 Try a funny walk on your heels, or your toes, or both. Add lots of funny, big arm, shoulder and head movements.

4 Clowns do lots of balancing on one foot and then suddenly stumble, nearly falling down as

they do little running steps to save themselves. Show me your funny balance shapes and your wobbling, stumbling quick steps to balance still again.

5 Sometimes they do lose balance and sit down on to their bottom. Show me a balance on your bottom with legs stuck up in the air.

6 Now twist over on to your tummy and show me another funny balance, with arms and legs lifted and doing swimming actions.

DANCE • THE CLOWNS – 10 minutes

1 Practise a pattern of funny walks, funny balances, staggers and runs to save yourself, and funny stumbles into a balance on bottom, chest, or both. Then jump up like Jack-In-The-Box.

2 Find a partner and pretend your partner needs cheering up. Find a good space as your little circus ring. One of you sit down as a spectator. The other one does his or her clown dance to include: funny walking, funny balancing, wobbling, staggering, and then a sit down and funny balance on bottom or front, or both.

3 Well done. Have one more practice. You can use our '8:4:2' pattern if you like – 8 funny walks; 4 funny balances, wobbles and staggering about; and 2 balances, 1 on bottom, 1 on chest.

4 Hands up all the spectators who laughed because you were amused. Can anyone tell me what you thought was good fun?

5 Change over now to a new clown and a new spectator. Start when you are ready. Clowns, dancers, give us a good laugh, please.

Year 2 | Lesson 2 30 minutes

Theme Friendships

WARM-UP ACTIVITIES – 7 minutes

1 Skip to this jazzy music for eight counts, then change direction and off you go again for 8 counts. Skip, 2, 3, 4, 5, 6, change direction; skip, 2, 3, 4, 5, 6, change again; skip, 2, 3, 4, 5, 6, 7, stop!

2 Now we are going to add meeting and giving a friendly hand touch to someone coming towards you, saying, 'Hello! Hello!' Ready? Keep thinking! Skip, 2, 3, 4, 5, 6, change direction; skip, 2, 3, 4, 5, meet, and 'Hello! Hello!'; skip, 2, 3, 4, 5, 6, change direction; skip, 2, 3, 4, 5, 'Hello! Hello!'

DANCE • FRIENDSHIPS – 23 minutes

1 This is your last month in infant school. Can you think about the time you started school, maybe not knowing anyone. Show me how you might have walked, skipped, run or galloped round the playground, all by yourself. Everything looked big and strange and you played by yourself. Off you go.

2 Walk in and out of one another, looking at those coming towards you. Show me a friendly gesture that you can make as you pass near someone. You can smile, nod your head or wave.

3 When I beat the drum, stop and make a friendly contact with the nearest person. It can be flat hand to hand; a handshake; a friendly touch on the shoulder; elbow to elbow; or two hands to two hands.

4 As you grew older you became good at playing with others. Find a partner you like to be with. Sit down and decide what shared activity you enjoy doing – throwing and catching; skipping with one rope; follow my leader; skipping side by side; walking, arm in arm; or dancing about together. Decide. Stand. Practise. Go!

5 You have done lots of moving together in this hall in our dance lessons. I think that all the moving and working together has helped to make you the brilliant, friendly class that you now are. All join hands in a big, friendly, class circle.

'Let's join hands, getting all together, (arms swinging)
Let's join hands in a circle round,
In we skip, good friends together, (four skips into centre)
Clap our hands and turn around. (clapping, turning on the spot)

Hands joined again, keeping close together, (facing out)
Skipping back out, off we go, (back to big circle places)
Our joined-up hands swing high and low, (in the big circle)
Now we shake hands (with own partner) and say "Hello!"'

PRACTICE   PERFORMANCE   COMMENTS   IMPROVEMENT   PRAISE AND THANKS

Year 3

Lesson 1 30 minutes

Theme Winter

WARM-UP ACTIVITIES – 5 minutes

January is often the coldest month. Let's pretend we are coming to school and moving to keep warm. Please join in the singing:

> 'This is the way we rub and run
>   (fast little steps and quick rubbing of chest, upper arms, shoulders),
> rub and run, rub and run,
> This is the way we rub and run on a cold and frosty morning.

This is the way we walk and shake
  (quick, lively big shakes of legs and arms),
walk and shake, walk and shake,
This is the way we walk and shake on a cold and frosty morning.'

(Repeat, then invite suggestions for other actions from the class, e.g. 'Hug me and skip'; 'Shake and bounce'; 'Bend and stretch'.)

MOVEMENT SKILLS TRAINING – 15 minutes

1 Each of my two cards has three winter words for you to think about, before deciding which set of words to choose.

Card 1 (Stream) RUSH FREEZE SKATE

Card 2 (Snow) FLOAT DRIFT MELT

2 What kind of movement does the rushing stream make you think of? Bubbling and splashing; hurrying and spreading; sometimes crashing over stones. Show me your rushing.

3 Will the 'Freeze' be sudden or gradual? Gradual, becoming smoother, steadier, firmer, still, hard, jagged. Rush for three or four seconds, then start your freezing. Go!

4 Well done, frozen streams. Skating can be performed expertly with never a stumble, or inexpertly with lots of wobbly arm waving. Brilliantly or wobbly ... off you go!

5 Snowflakes now. Can you tell me how they float down? Lightly; gently; fluttering; then softly landing. Show me how you might slowly float, going from space to space, before coming to rest.

6 Those were excellent, gentle, snowflake movements. Well done. If your snowflake is suddenly struck by a strong wind, how will it respond and drift? High and low; with changes of direction, with pauses between gusts; with sudden, fast movements; all before settling, still, in a snowflake shape. Ready for the wind? Drift!

7 When the snow melts into a puddle on the ground, it will be a slow and smooth movement, spreading outwards. Start in your snowflake shape, with parts of your body off the floor. Now melt slowly.

DANCE • WINTER WORDS– 10 minutes

1 Hands up the 'stream words' group. Hands up the 'snowflakes' group.

2 Show me your starting shape which should tell me if you are going to rush or float – two very different actions.

3 I will call out the pairs of words to guide your timing. Rush or float ... freeze or drift... skate or melt...

4 Hold your final position, please, with the skaters in a clever or awkward position and shape.

Year 3 | Lesson 2 30 minutes

Theme Fast and slow

WARM-UP ACTIVITIES – 5 minutes

1 Can you be very clever and show me a leg action on the spot; then a short travel; then big body movements, like bending, stretching, twisting, rising or lowering, on the spot?

2 Show me your starting position for your first action, with arms, legs and body nicely balanced and ready. Begin!

3 Stop! Now look for a good space for your short travelling action. I hope it's different from the first action. Go!

4 Stop! On the spot, show me your one or two whole body movements.

5 Stop in a held shape. Well done. Keep practising all three actions in your own time. Show me your still shape at the start and finish, each time. Off you go!

MOVEMENT SKILLS TRAINING – 10 minutes

1 Stand ready, again, for your first leg action on the spot. Pretend the floor is hot and do the action as fast as you can. Go!

2 Stop! Now, do your travelling action at equally high speed to take you to a space. Make every part of your body join in.

3 On the spot, find a good balance position for your high speed body movements – up and down, in and out, round and back, go!

4 Wow! You looked like out-of-control machines. Well done. Now, like machines with almost no power, do your three actions in ultra-slow motion, just moving and no more. Slow mo ... go!

5 Use your joints fully to make your slow motion a whole body slow motion. Don't cut down on the size of your actions. Once again, v-e-e-r-y slo-o-ow-ly, begin!

DANCE • FAST FORWARD, FAST BACK, SLOW MOTION REPLAY – 15 minutes

1 Find a partner. I want you both to think about a favourite TV sport that you might perform in an unusual dance.

2 Performers, show me by your starting shape what your sport is. I see swimmers, athletes, cricketers, golfers, footballers, tennis and netball players, weight lifters, canoeists, gliders and jockeys.

3 Practise your chosen sport and make a little repeating pattern of three or four parts that is easy to remember (e.g. jump, catch, run in and score; or forehand, backhand, run in and smash).

4 One of you stand ready to perform. Partner, sit down. Pretend you are about to watch sport on TV. As you press the control buttons, say 'Normal' or 'Fast forward' or 'Fast back' or 'Slow motion', and your sporty partner must immediately respond. Be sensible, please, and don't use 'Fast back' or 'Fast forward' for more than a few seconds. Operators ... begin.

5 Stop! Sportspersons, sit down beside your operators and tell them how you would like them to change their button pushing to help you perform better.

6 Same dancers and operators. One more improved practice, please.

7 Well done, everyone. That looked much better. Now change duties and we'll do the whole thing again twice.

8 Each half of the class can now enjoy watching the other half.

Year 4 | Lesson 1 30 minutes

Theme Awareness of space

WARM-UP ACTIVITIES – 5 minutes

1 As you travel from space to space to my shaking tambourine, use some of the actions we have used in our lessons – gallop, slide, rush, creep, float, leap or hurry. Perform short travels and stop on the loud beat of the tambourine. Go!

2 Use your eyes while you are still to look for the next good space. Varied travelling actions, please. Go!

3 On each stop, show me a balanced, whole body shape where parts of you reach out into the spaces in front, above, to the sides and behind.

4 Well done travellers and reachers into space.

MOVEMENT SKILLS TRAINING – 15 minutes

1 Stand in your own space and note exactly where you are. Show me how your clever feet can travel away from your spot and return to the same place sixteen counts later. Go! 1, 2, 3, 4 (up to) 14, 15, 16 and still!

2 Let's try again. Show me your varied actions and all the parts of the hall that you can visit in sixteen counts. Go!

3 As well as visiting many parts of the room, can you reach out and touch the space around you, at different levels (high leaps, low slithering, medium arm swings)?

4 Now show me how many movements you can do in sixteen counts without moving away from your spot on the floor. Arms, legs, head, shoulders and back can all bend, stretch, twist, reach, swing into all the spaces surrounding you.

5 Some movements, like a long stretch, can be slow, taking several counts. Others can swing or reach out quickly into space. Play around with the speeds of your big body movements.

DANCE • SPACE TRAVEL – 10 minutes

1 Find a partner and decide who will be number one and who will be number two.

2 While I sound out sixteen counts, number one will move on the spot and number two will travel through space. Both will finish, still, in an attractive shape. Ready? Begin.

3 1, 2, 3 ... 13, 14, 15 and be still. Show me your firm shape.

4 Now number two will move on the spot and number one will travel. Be together again on count sixteen. Go! 1, 2, 3 ... 15 and be still.

5 Let's look at our partner's actions on the spot, and then travelling. One can perform while the other watches. This will help you to plan actions that are different to your partner's for variety.

6 Now, we'll do the whole thing twice through, working together.

7 Half of the class will watch the other half. Look for and tell me about neat, varied movements and any really good examples of travelling for sixteen counts, exactly.

DEMONSTRATIONS   *REFLECTIONS*   *FURTHER PRACTICE*   *IMPROVEMENT*

Year 4 | Lesson 2 30 minutes

Theme Gestures

WARM-UP ACTIVITIES – 5 minutes

1 March smartly for eight counts, turn on the spot, march for four counts, then make four quick waves to four different classmates. Do not speak. Let your body gestures speak for you. 'Hello!' 'Hi!' Marching, turning, gesturing, go!

March smartly, 3, 4, 5, 6, 7, now turn; turn, 2, 3, 4; wave, 2, 3, 4; march briskly, swing your arms, 5, 6, 7, 8; turn, turn, turn, turn; 'Hello! Hello!', 3, 4; again.

MOVEMENT SKILLS TRAINING – 15 minutes

1 Gesturing is like speaking with your body. Big gestures after a 'Goal!' are seen every week on TV. Use your body to tell me that your team has just scored a 'Goal!'

2 Try it on the spot: walk into it, bringing your punching arm from behind to high in front, or do a leap on the spot.

3 Try one in slow motion with a long arm pull from behind.

4 Show me the kind of gesture a goalkeeper might make if poor defending caused the goal. Stamping foot? Clenched fist?

5 Later in the game the referee refuses all demands by team A for a penalty kick. How will team A gesture towards the hated referee? Will they point a finger threateningly? Punch a clenched fist?

6 A team A player is so cheeky towards the referee that he is sent off in disgrace. Show me how the referee and all team B might signal 'Off!' to the player who is reluctant to go. Will it be one arm pointing to the changing rooms? Or a hand on hips, head high, look of disgust?

DANCE • GESTURES – 10 minutes

1 Well done. You did gesture and say things to me without saying a word.

2 Find a partner. Decide who will be asking a favour by gesturing to say 'Please!' or 'You must!' or 'I need it!' or 'Please! I'm desperate!' or 'Give it to me, or else!'

3 The other partner replies using gestures, saying 'No!' or 'You must be joking!' or 'Go away!'

4 You can pretend to be two friends, or parent and child. It's going to be a one minute struggle to see who wears out the other person with greater determination. Get started, please.

5 One person can walk away at one point and be pursued and confronted by the other one, pleading. Keep struggling, everyone!

6 Let's look at lots of these gesturing duos, and see who we think are the winners. Look out for any surprising gestures, please.

Year 5

Theme Contrasting actions

WARM-UP ACTIVITIES – 5 minutes

1 Tiptoe silently, pretending someone is asleep and you mustn't waken them. Tiny, little, gentle steps. Shhhhh!

2 Pretend the floor is a drum now, and you want your loud, heavy beating to be heard above all the others. Go! Bang! Bang! Bang!

3 Travel with your feet never leaving the floor as you slide, slither, glide along the surface, making very little sound.

4 Now the floor is hot and you leap and bound to keep high above it. Bounce and bounce and leap up high.

MOVEMENT SKILLS TRAINING – 12 minutes

1 In addition to the gentle and strong, light and heavy contrasts we have practised, we can use speed and direction change contrasts. Think of a favourite travelling action, using feet.

2 As I call out 'Normal!' or 'Slow motion!' or 'Fast forward!' or 'Direction!', can you change the speed or direction of your action? Ready? Normal ... fast forward ... slow motion ... normal ... direction ... fast forward ... normal ... slow motion ... stop!

3 Well done. Your responses were immediate and very contrasting.

4 Can you make a pattern with two pairs of opposites? Aim for variety as well as contrasts. For example, can your changes include actions, body shape, direction, speed or force?

5 The medium-speed music is quick enough for stepping and travelling, but slow enough for turns, gestures and big body movements with its 1, 2, 3, 4; opposite, 2, 3, 4 rhythm. Begin.

DANCE • OPPOSITES – 13 minutes

1 Well done. I saw many good examples of 'Opposites'. Find a partner and take turns at showing each other your four-part sequence with its two pairs of opposites.

2 Partners, can you now plan a four-part sequence, using the best of your two routines, ideally with a good and varied mixture?

3 Keep practising and chant out the nature of the opposites. For example, 'Slow and soft, on the spot; quick and strong, travelling; rise and open, 3, 4; lower and close, 3, 4.'

4 If you prefer, you can repeat each half of your pattern to make your sequence last longer.

5 Finally, decide if you will perform the movement together; or have one do the first movement alone with the other showing the opposite and contrasting movement alone. Working alone can be interesting with one on the spot, the other travelling around the stationary one.

6 Let's have each half watching the other half to look out for and identify imaginative ideas and neat performances.

7 Thank you for your varied, interesting demonstrations and friendly, helpful comments. Let's have more practice so that you can include some of the good ideas seen and praised to help improve your performance.

Year 5

Lesson 2 30 minutes

Theme Vocal sounds as accompaniment and stimulus for movement

WARM-UP ACTIVITIES – 5 minutes

1 We can accompany dance with recorded music, instruments, body part sounds such as clapping, and voice sounds. Follow me as I travel all round the room and accompany me with your good voice sounds, copying my actions. A helpful rhythm will be appreciated.

2 I liked the 'Toom, toom, toom, toom' with my marching; the 'Tick, tock, tick, tock' with my slow, feet astride stepping; the loud humming as I turned; and the 'Boomp, boomp, boomp, boomp' with my bouncing.

MOVEMENT SKILLS TRAINING – 10 minutes

1 Find a partner and decide who is the mover and who is the voice accompaniment. Mover, can you vary your actions, staying on the spot only? Do small, smooth movements for a small, smooth, continuous sound from your partner.

2 Now try a bigger action, which might be a stop/start to invite a louder, jerky, on/off sound.

3 Rise and fall, mover, to give your partner an interesting variety of sounds to make. Changing speed would be good to see and hear.

4 Change places, please. The new mover will travel, not too far or fast, with the sound-making partner travelling and making some brilliant, unique sounds.

5 Travelling partner, vary your actions to include some slow, smooth, jerky, big, small movements to give your sound-making partner lots of variety, making sounds never heard before.

6 Let's have each half of the class performing and sound making for the other half. Watch and listen for brilliant partnerships to tell me about, so that we can share really good ideas.

DANCE • VOICE SOUNDS – 15 minutes

1 Form groups of five. Sit down and discuss a favourite idea for a holiday 'Voice Sounds' dance. You may elongate or shorten action words (PI-a-a-a-ay te-e-e-enis); place names (R-i-v-i-era); favourite food (Ba-a-a-a-nan-a split); or invent sounds or words to accompany your holiday actions.

2 Think of an enjoyable holiday sporting action; a favourite resort; or food, glorious food. Decide, then work out your accompanying actions as a group.

3 Sporting action will be represented by the actions, ultra slow, normal speed or speeded up, if you can shorten the word.

4 Place names and food can be accompanied by an interesting mixture of travelling, jumping, turning, rising, falling, gesturing and stillness – long, drawn out, normal speed or accelerated to make it eye-catching and funny.

5 Agree your starting shapes and finishing shapes as a group.

6 Try to include actions that make a short, repeating pattern to help you to remember them easily. Keep practising.

7 For your demonstrations, one group at a time, try to express 'Our choice of sport, or resort, or food, is the best – just like our movement. Watch our larger than life actions and listen to our super sounds.'

Year 6

Lesson 1 30 minutes

Theme Winter

WARM-UP ACTIVITIES – 5 minutes

1 With a partner, do 'Follow my Leader' where the leader shows lively travelling actions that use every joint to warm you up. Keep in time with the medium-speed music. Go!

2 Stop! The other partner will now lead in whole body, lively actions on the spot. Use every joint and muscle. Begin!

3 In your two-part, winter warm-up, travel to a good space, then face each other for your on the spot actions. Keep with the phrasing of the music as you do your repeating pattern.

MOVEMENT SKILLS TRAINING – 15 minutes

1 Your deep breathing and perspiring faces tell me that you warmed up well. Well done. Collect a piece of percussion and one of my three sets of cards with their three winter words.

Set 1	Birds in winter wind		
	FLUTTER	SOAR	SWIRL
Set 2	Snow		
	DRIFT	FREEZE	MELT
Set 3	People		
	STAMP	SLIP	SHIVER

2 Put your card down on the floor. Study the words and plan how your movements will clearly represent the words.

3 Number one dancer, practise your three actions clearly for your partner to watch. Start when ready, without any percussion.

4 Dancer, your partner will give you one helpful comment to improve your performance. Were the actions correct? Were the shapes clear? Was the timing too hurried or too slow?

5 Same dancer again, please, accompanied by partner on percussion. Percussionist, quietly accompany your partner, starting and stopping each time to make the three actions separate.

6 Well done. The improvements were obvious. Now change places.

7 New dancers, stand ready, please. No accompaniment yet as partner watches to see what might be improved. Begin when ready.

8 Dancers, your partner will tell you one thing that might be improved. Can the main movement feature be expressed better? What about an exciting contrast in speed or effort?

9 Same dancers with percussion this time. Each action is started and stopped by the percussion. Start when ready, please.

10 Well done dancers and partners whose advice produced an obvious improvement.

DANCE • WINTER WORDS WITH PERCUSSION – 10 minutes

1 I have placed your couple next to a couple with a different set of winter words. Hide your card so they can't read the words.

2 Each couple in turn will perform twice, working as dancer and percussionist to see if the other couple recognise the actions.

3 Do it all again. Observers, please watch and then tell the other couple what you particularly liked in their demonstration.

Year 6 Lesson 2 30 minutes

Theme Rhythmic patterns

WARM-UP ACTIVITIES – 6 minutes

1 Show me your best stepping in time with this medium-speed music. When I beat the drum loudly on count eight each time, can you introduce a change – style or size of step, body shape or direction, for example? Best stepping, go! Best stepping, spacing well, 5, 6, 7 and change! Keep practising.

2 Well done. I saw changes of step size; stepping with high knees; stepping and closing sideways; sliding; and feet apart stepping.

3 Leaping is like high, wide running or stepping. Do four lively leaps, then four 'easy' actions on the spot. Go! Leap and leap and leap for 4; on the spot, 3, 4.

4 I liked your contrasting big/lively and small/easy movements.

MOVEMENT SKILLS TRAINING – 12 minutes

1 Still working in groups of eight counts, can you stay on the spot and show me a pattern of favourite actions or movements? May I suggest stepping, bouncing, skipping, clapping, gesturing, turning? Two or more actions, neatly linked and contrasting, will be excellent. Go! On the spot, on the spot, 5, 6, 7 and change; new action, contrast action, 5, 6, 7, again!

2 Well done. That looked really good and I enjoyed the many shapes as you put your whole body into it.

3 Now for favourite travelling actions. We have used steps and leaps of all sorts. You might want to add skipping, bouncing, running and galloping. Can you show me your varied travelling pattern with eight counts to each one? Go! Travel, 2, 3, 4, 5, 6, 7, change; new travel, 3, 4, 5, 6, change again!

DANCE • PATTERNS ON A STAGE – 12 minutes

1 The middle third of the hall is going to be your stage for the final part of our lesson. It extends from side to side.

2 Start off the stage. Walk to the edge of the stage and then do a two-part travelling action pattern to take you on to the stage. On the spot, you will then do your two-part pattern. Then make your way off stage to the other end with the same, or a different, two-part travelling action pattern.

3 While you are waiting, off stage, look for a good space before you come on stage again to repeat your three patterns – the travelling on stage; the on the spot; and the travelling from the stage.

4 I will stand at the side of your stage to watch your on-stage performance. Pretend I am a talent scout and do your very best.

5 Each half of the class will now watch the other half from the side of the stage. Spectators, you may quietly clap any impressive performance as the dancer leaves the stage, and be able to tell us what you particularly liked about him or her.

6 Spectators, look for neat movements using the whole body in larger than life activity; good, clear, proud body shapes; and varied use of directions and body tension, both firm and gentle.

STAGES IN CREATING AND PROGRESSING A DANCE

First of all, decide what the dance will be about, for example, autumn leaves, making a puppet, or fireworks.

Stage 1

a *Decide which actions, neatly performed, will be used to represent the subject and express it in movement.*

Autumn leaves hover, float, glide, rise, fall, tilt and turn, and finally sink to the ground.

Puppets move in a floppy, loose way, as if they have no muscles, only bones that move jerkily as if pulled by strings.

Fireworks include rockets whooshing into flight, sparklers sending out their sparks, and bangers jumping noisily and unexpectedly.

b *Decide how best to use body parts and shapes to make the actions look poised, neat, correct and well-controlled.*

The whole body makes the shape of autumn leaves which include parts curling in, parts sticking out, some smooth, some crinkly.

The puppet's arms can lift jerkily and alternately, as if pulled up straight by strings, then drop to bend and flop again.

The firework rocket is represented by both arms reaching forward to make a long, streamlined shape.

Stage 2

Decide how to use the whole room space, as if it is a stage, to make the dance more interesting and exciting.

Autumn leaves soar from low to high, turn in the same space, hover, hardly moving, glide to a far corner, drop to the ground.

Puppets, learning how to move, experiment by using hands and arms to reach out into space in front, to the sides, behind and overhead.

Fireworks are interesting with the contrasting actions of the rocket's straight whoosh, the Catherine wheel's spinning, and the unpredictable zig-zag jumping and shifting of the bangers.

Stage 3

Consider how the performance might be made more attractive, surprising and expressive by applying just the right amount of speed and force.

The slow, gentle rise and fall of autumn leaves, still attached to their branches, contrasts with the sudden, almost explosive snap and break away from the branch.

Puppets can swing and circle arms gently and slowly, and then punch the air firmly and strongly.

With fireworks, the long, smooth, ongoing rocket zoom contrasts with its eventual sudden, explosive, fragmented scattering.

Stage 4

How do we relate to others in our dance?

Even if 'Autumn Leaves' is an individual dance, we share the space unselfishly with others as we weave, swoop, soar, hover, glide, tilt and turn, in and out, alongside or around them.

In a 'Puppet Maker' dance, the puppet and its maker mirror each other in learning ways to move, and in leading and following.

In a 'Fireworks' dance, the pupils start one group at a time. 'Sparklers, begin! Bangers, get ready, begin! Sparklers, keep going! Rockets, ready ... go! Sparklers, bangers, rockets, all stop now.

AN EXAMPLE OF TEACHING A FOUR-STAGE DANCE PROGRESSION

For 'The Snake' dance the class is in lines of four behind a leader. The snake's actions ripple from the leader (the head), down the body to the end person. Team members copy the gradually changing actions of the one in front and then pass them on.

Music Medium to fast and jazzy to accompany the brisk steps, skips, jumps, bounces, claps and gestures which are typically included.

What actions? What use of body parts? What shapes?

STAGE 1 • LESSON 1 • WHAT IS YOUR SNAKE DOING?

a Leaders, change the action when you think everyone has picked it up. Can you include two or three interesting, contrasting actions?

b What are your feet doing? They can stay together or apart, pass each other normally, or each can swing across or behind.

c Can you change body shape to add more variety (e.g. long, stretched on tiptoes, stepping; wide arms and feet bouncing; skipping with knees and arms bending)?

STAGE 2 • LESSON 2 • WHERE IS YOUR SNAKE DOING ITS ACTIONS?

a New leaders, give your snake lots of space as you visit all parts of the room, revising the two or three actions used last week. If the way ahead is suddenly crowded, dance on the spot.

b Action on the spot, maybe with clapping and turning, is worth including as a contrast to lively travelling.

c Can you include a direction change somewhere? This looks good if you change action at the same time (e.g. step forward, 3, 4; bounce to side, 3, 4; step forward, 3, 4; bounce sideways, 3, 4).

STAGE 3 • LESSON 3 • HOW IS YOUR SNAKE MOVING?

What speed? What force, effort, tension?

a New leader, revise the two or three contrasting actions your snake has been practising. I am looking for neat actions and clear body shapes, sometimes with a direction change, please.

b Can you now introduce a speed change? You can be a slow motion snake, then speed ahead.

Which of your actions suits a slow performance? Which helps you to move ahead more quickly?

c Can your snake's style change from being smooth, gliding, silent, neat, to being awkward, clumping, noisy?

STAGE 4 • LESSON 4 • HOW DO YOUR SNAKE PARTS RELATE TO ONE ANOTHER?

Leading, following, side by side? Touching or apart?

a All discuss any other formation your group might like to use. Must you always be one behind the other in a straight line?

b Your group of four can make a diamond shape, 1:2:1. You can be lightly joined at some point. You could be two by two.

c Practise with the music, then we'll have demonstrations by each snake in turn to share ideas for neat, varied actions with clear shapes; good use of space; contrasts of speed or effort; and ideas for the way you relate to one another and work together.

TRADITIONAL DANCE STEPS

English and Scottish country dancing, with their easy steps and figures, easily obtained music, and potential for being used creatively, provide enjoyable, sociable and very physical lessons. Traditional dances have a long 'shelf life', and are popular because everyone is involved for about three minutes, all doing the same thing.

English country dance steps include:

1 *Dance-walk*, the natural, everyday action of going from foot to foot, with a springy lift before each step. The travelling foot stays near the ground. 'Step, bounce; step, lift; step, spring.'

2 *Skipping or Hop-Stepping* comes naturally to young children, and is similar to dance-walk, but the whole body springs clear of the floor with each step. 'Step, hop; step, spring; step, lift; and lift.'

3 *The Side-Step* is a sideways step with one foot, and a quick catch up with the other foot. This is called 'chasse', when done slowly, for example when holding hands with a partner and side stepping to the centre of a circle, then out again. When done quickly, it is called the 'gallop' step, for example when in a circle with all members travelling to the left for eight, then to the right for eight.

4 *The Polka or Double Step* is a 1, 2, 3 and hop, very fast, springy step on the balls of the feet without the heels touching the floor. '1, 2, 3, and hop; step, step, step and hop; step, close,

step and hop.' With a partner, it can be danced round in circles, completing half a turn on each '1, 2, 3 and hop.'

Scottish country dance steps include:

1 *Skip Change of Step or Travelling Step*. Step forward with the right foot. Bring the left foot up behind the right foot. Step forward with the right foot. Now repeat with the left foot leading. 'Left, 2, 3; right, 2, 3.' Now add a hop at the start and the step becomes 'Hop, step together, step; hop, 1, 2, 3; lift, right, 2, 3; lift, left, 2, 3.' For the hop, the leading leg is straight and raised only a few inches off the floor.

2 *Slipping Step* is used in circles where all join hands to circle with quick step-close action, eight to the left and eight to the right, as in the quick gallop step sideways of English country dancing.

3 *Pas de Basque or Setting Step* is difficult, with its long beat and two shorter ones. Step to the right with the right foot, close the left to the right, then mark time on the spot with the right foot. Step left, close, beat; step right, mark time. When the class can do this we add in a jump into the first step. 'Jump to right, 2, 3; jump, left, 2, 3.' Knee and ankle of the opposite leg are stretched as weight goes on to each foot. This extended leg is carried round and down so that the step is done on the spot, not from side to side. 'Jump, 2, 3 and stretch; jump, 2, 3 and reach.'

TRADITIONAL DANCE FIGURES

Traditional dances and 'creative traditional' dances are made by linking figures in a repeating pattern. Each of the four figures of a typical, 32-bar dance, with an A:B:C:D pattern, will take eight bars of the music. An attraction of the creative form is the ability to simplify the pattern to a two-figure, repeating A:B:A:B pattern, and to add your own figures to the class, traditional-style dance repertoire.

One-couple Figures

Stage

1	2	1	2	1	2
1	2	1	2	1	2

Couples stand two metres apart across the room. The 'top of set' is the end of the room nearer the music and usually the stage end from which most of the teaching is done. As couples face the top end, the partner on the left is number 1, the boy's position, and the other is number 2, the girl's position. Each figure takes eight counts of the music.

1 *Round partner and back*. Partner 1 dances round in front of partner 2, and back to own place for four counts. Partner 2 dances round in front of partner 1 and back to own place for four counts.

2 *Advance, retire, change places*. Both dance towards each other with two skipping steps, then back to places with two skipping steps. Both travel towards each other, take right hands and change places for four counts.

3 *Repeat 2* back to own places, giving left hands.

4 *Down the middle and up again, or 'Promenade'*. Both move in, join right hands and face bottom of set. They dance for four counts, turn and go back to own places for four counts.

5 *Change places and back again*. Give right hand to partner and turn partner into your place for four counts. Return to own places, giving left hand, for four counts.

6 *Cast off on own side*. Facing top of set, cast off to own side (partner 1 turns to left, partner 2 turns to right) and dance to bottom of set for four counts. Give partner right hand and dance up to top of set to own places for four counts.

7 *Back to back or Do-Si-Do*. Move forward towards partner, passing right shoulders and back, passing left shoulders, dancing round each other, four counts to each direction.

8 *Side with partner*. Both move forward to right, passing left shoulders. Half turn, anti-clockwise, to face each other. Move sideways to left back to places, turning clockwise to face each other (side left and side right).

Two-couple figures

Stage

B1	G1	B1	G1	B1	G1
B2	G2	B2	G2	B2	G2

In two couple sets, the couple nearer the top of the set is the first couple. B1 is first boy, G1 is first girl. The couple further from the top is the second couple. B2 is second boy, G2 is second girl. Each figure takes eight counts of the music.

1 *Circle left and right*. Hands are joined with partner and dancer beside you. Eight slipping steps are danced to the left, then eight back to right to starting places.

2 *Wheel or right and left hand star*. Right hand is given to dancer diagonally opposite, first boy with second girl, and first girl with second boy. Perform four skipping steps, then back to own places with left hands joined for four counts.

3 *Cast off to own side*, followed by second couple. First boy turns to left, first girl to right to cast off and go behind line of set. Second couple follow to top of set, then cast off as they follow first couple to bottom of set for four counts. Couples turn in, meet with right hands joined to return up middle of set to starting places. Progression to let second couple become first can be achieved by first couple making an arch at bottom of set for second couple to go under as they lead to top.

4 *Rights and lefts*. Change places with your partner, giving right hands, with two travelling steps. Stay on partner's side and give left hand to change places with one of the other couple, two steps. Cross set to own side, giving right hand to partner for two counts. Return to own places, giving left hand to one of opposite couple, counts 7 and 8. (Round a square – cross set; move along opposite side; cross set; back to own places, two travelling steps to each side.)

5 *Figure-of-eight round second couple*. First couple cross over to go behind second couple into partner's place, for four counts. Cross over behind second couple back to own place, for four counts. Progression to let second couple change places can be done on last two counts by a side step by second couple to first place.

6 *Under the arches*. Couples face each other, up and down the set, with nearer hands joined. First couple advance and go under the arch made by raised arms of second couple, for four counts. They turn to face each other again, and this time second couple go under the high arch made by first couple, for four counts.

7 *Setting and changing sides*. All do two setting steps to own partner, then change sides with two travelling steps, giving right hands. Set for two again, cross back to own places, giving left hands.

Traditional Folk Dance Lesson Plan

The 30-minute lesson includes:

WARMING-UP ACTIVITIES – 5 minutes

These varied steps can relate to the new figures to be taught, or they can be travelling steps or steps on the spot of any kind, to stimulate quick, easy, enjoyable action to put the class in the mood for dance. The warm-up can be done alone or with a partner. As well as inspiring action, the teacher establishes high standards of neat footwork and good, safe, unselfish sharing of space.

TEACH FIGURES OF NEW DANCE – 14 minutes

Teaching is easiest in a big circle formation where all can see and copy the teacher. Often, all can perform the whole dance together, slowly and carefully, figure by figure, practising it to the teacher's voice, then doing it at the correct speed to music.

Teaching in sets of two, three, four or more couples is more difficult because the sets are separate, often with someone's back to the teacher. Each leading couple in turn will be taken slowly through the figures, walking, then dancing them to the music or the teacher's vocal accompaniment.

TEACH THE NEW DANCE – 7 minutes

Ideally, the new dance will be performed without stopping, helped by early reminders to the next dancers from the teacher. It is sometimes necessary to stop the music after each dancing couple has completed the dance, because of problems experienced by some of the dancers. The new couples are put in position, ready, the music is re-started, and they do the dance once through.

REVISE A FAVOURITE DANCE – 4 minutes

This last dance, often chosen by pupils, should be a contrast to the lesson's new dance for variety. A lively circle dance with all pupils dancing non-stop can be contrasted with a set dance where only two of the four couples are dancing at a time.

A more experienced teacher's 30-minute lesson plan can include:

Warming-up activities	4 minutes
Revision of new dance learned in previous lesson	6 minutes
Teach steps and figures of new dance	10 minutes
Dance new dance	6 minutes
Revise a favourite, well-known dance	4 minutes

Traditional Dance

SUITABLE FOR INFANTS AND JUNIORS

WARMING-UP ACTIVITIES – 5 minutes

1 Skip by yourself, feeling the eight-count phrasing of the music. Can you change direction as you start a new count of eight? Skip, 2, 3, 4, 5, 6, change direction. Travel, 2, 3, 4, 5, 6, change again.

2 This time, skip quietly and neatly for six counts, then gently touch hands with someone coming towards you, on 7 and 8. Skip, 2, 3, 4, 5, 6, clap and clap. Skip, 2, 3, 4, 5, 6, meet and clap.

TEACH FIGURES OF NEW DANCE • THE MUFFIN MAN – 14 minutes

With a partner in a circle, all face centre, hands joined. Boy is on left of partner.

1 All dance to centre and back, twice, four dance-walks to each advance and retire. Forward, 2, 3, 4; back, 2, 3, again. Forward, 2, 3, 4; back, 2, face your partner.

2 Face partner and take both hands. Two chasse steps sideways to centre and back (or four gallop steps each way with younger pupils) and

repeat. Step to side, close feet, step in, close feet; step out, close feet, step out, close feet.

3 Promenade partners anti-clockwise round the circle with dance walk. Boy is on inside of circle. Partners' left and right hands are joined.

4 Swing partners, pivoting quickly on right foot, pushing with left or, more slowly and easily, walking round in a circle with nearer feet close together.

DANCE NEW DANCE • THE MUFFIN MAN (ENGLISH) – 7 minutes

Music The Muffin Man or any 32-bar jig.

Formation Big circle with partners.

Bars 1–8 All dance to centre and back, twice.

Bars 9–16 Face partner, taking both hands and perform two chasse steps to centre and back. (Younger dancers, four gallop steps each way.) Repeat.

Bars 17–24 Promenade partners in anti-clockwise circle.

Bars 25–32 Swing partners.

Keep repeating.

REVISE A FAVOURITE DANCE – 4 minutes

To provide variety and contrast, it is recommended that this dance is a well-known, popular traditional dance, ideally in sets, or a more modern, created dance.

Traditional Dance 30 minutes

SUITABLE FOR INFANTS AND JUNIORS

WARMING-UP ACTIVITIES – 5 minutes

1 Follow your leader, about two metres apart, copying your leader's actions, including clapping hands. The phrasing of the music is in groups of eight counts to help you time your actions.

2 New leader, can you include one or more of the actions already practised, and try to add some contrasting actions (e.g. quiet walking; lively skipping; chasse left; chasse right; polka round)?

TEACH FIGURES OF NEW DANCE • PAT-A-CAKE-POLKA – 14 minutes

Partners in a double circle, with boys on inside of circle, holding both hands of partner, ready to dance anti-clockwise.

1 With foot on anti-clockwise side, both dance 'Heel and toe' on the spot, then polka step quickly to boy's left, 1, 2, 3. (Left, right, left.) Repeat back to boy's right, 'Heel, toe, 1, 2, 3.'
   Repeat all of this quick movement. Heel, toe, polka step left; heel, toe, polka step right.

2 Partners face each other and clap right hands three times, rapidly; clap left hands three times rapidly; clap both hands three times, and then clap own knees three times. Left, 2, 3; right, 2, 3; both, 2, 3; knees, 2, 3.

3 Boys turn partner with an elbow or both hands, swing round to finish facing each other, ready to start again.

DANCE NEW DANCE • PAT-A-CAKE-POLKA (ENGLISH) – 7 minutes

Formation Double circle, with boys' backs to centre. Directions given are those for the boy or dancer on inside of circle.

Counts 1–2 Heel and toe, polka step (fast chasse) left.

Counts 3–4 Heel and toe, polka step right.

Counts 5–8 Repeat all the above, to left and to right.

Counts 9–12 Partners clap right hands three times; left hands three times; both hands three times; own knees three times.

Counts 13–16 Partners turn each other to starting positions to repeat the dance.

Repeat.

REVISE A FAVOURITE DANCE – 4 minutes

To provide variety and contrast, it is recommended that this dance is a less vigorously physical, traditional dance, or a more modern, created dance.

Creative Traditional Dance 30 minutes

SUITABLE FOR INFANTS AND JUNIORS

At a simple level of planned creativity within folk dance, the class is taught five or six traditional dance figures and then challenged to decide which four figures to include and the order in which to include them in their four-part, repeating dance.

WARMING-UP ACTIVITIES – 5 minutes

1 Dance on the spot for eight counts, then travel through good spaces for the next eight counts.

2 'On the spot' can include dance-walking, skipping, setting or even bouncing in time with the music. Let your travelling really go somewhere as a contrast. On the spot, 3, 4, 5, 6, 7, now travel; 1, 2, travelling well, 5, 6, now on the spot.

3 Find a partner. One of you show your dancing on the spot to the other and both remember it. Then the other partner show your travelling for both to practise and remember.

4 Decide whether to dance side by side, or following the leader, as you perform your shared dance.

TEACH ONE-COUPLE FIGURES TO BE LINKED CREATIVELY – 15 minutes

Partner on left as couple face top of set is boy or A. Partner on right is girl or B. Each figure takes eight bars of the music.

1 *Round partner and back*. A dances round in front of B and back to place, for four counts. B repeats round A, dancing for four counts.

2 *Cast off to own side*. A turns to left, B turns to right and they dance to bottom for four counts. Turn in, join nearer or right hands to dance to top and back to own places.

3 *Change places with partner*, for four counts, giving right hands, then four to change back to own places, giving left hands.

4 *Down middle of set*, for four counts, with nearer or right hands joined, turn and dance back to top and own places, for four counts.

5 *Back to back or Do-si-do*. Both go forward, passing right shoulders, and back, passing left shoulders, without turning body round, i.e. keep facing partner's side, for four counts each way.

COUPLES PLAN, CREATE AND PRACTISE OWN 32-BAR DANCE – 10 minutes

Each partner of the pair can select two of the above five figures he or she wishes to include in their four-figure dance. Both partners share in deciding the order of the figures to ensure a neat, smooth flow, figure to figure; variety in directions; in being joined or separate; and an ending that appeals to both.

Creative Traditional Dance   30 minutes

SUITABLE FOR INFANTS AND JUNIORS

The 'creative' element can extend beyond simple decisions on combining the several practised figures to create a four-figure dance. Pupils' own figures, planned, practised and enjoyed during the warming-up activities, can be included in the created dance.

WARMING-UP ACTIVITIES – 5 minutes

1 Follow your leader, two metres apart, copying leader's actions. Lead your partner into good spaces and include three or four neat, quiet, contrasting actions. (Contrast, for example, from small walking or running steps, hardly travelling; lively, skip change of step or polka with good travel; gentle bounces on the spot and lively, slipping steps sideways.)

2 New leader, keep the same actions, but try to include a change of direction and body shape somewhere. (For example, small steps, body stretched tall on tiptoes; lively, long skipping steps with well bent knees and arms; little bounces turning on the spot; chasse side steps to left and to right with arms and legs parting wide and closing.)

TEACH ONE-COUPLE FIGURES TO BE LINKED CREATIVELY – 15 minutes

Partner on left facing top is boy or A. Partner on right is girl or B. Each figure takes eight bars of the music.

1 *Cast off to own side*. A turns to left, B turns to right and dance to bottom for four counts, then turn in, meet, giving right or nearer hands and dance to top and own places for four counts.

2 *Advance and retire and change places*. Partners dance towards each other for two counts, then back for two, then they go forward, giving right hands to change places. Now in their partner's place, they usually repeat this figure, back to own places, but they can be challenged – 'How will you return to own places, taking four counts? The same way back or another way?'

3 *Round partner and back*. A dances round in front of B and back to place. B repeats round A and back to own place. The partner being danced round, do something on the spot as partner goes round (e.g. setting steps, turning to keep facing partner; or give a helping hand to partner, on count 3, round to his or her place.)

4 *Practise own eight-count, created figure* that develops from the warming-up activities (e.g. include one stationary and one travelling dancer; partners can part and close; or one on spot and one going round in a circle.)

COUPLES PLAN, CREATE AND PRACTISE OWN 32-BAR DANCE – 10 minutes

Couples may include one or two of their own ideas in the four-figure dance. The 'Advance and retire' with own ending, if chosen, will be half of the dance.

Half of the class demonstrate to the other half. 'Look out for and tell me about any brilliant ideas you see. Look for dancing in time with the music, and always being ready for the next figure.'

IMPROVING AND PROGRESSING TRADITIONAL DANCE

The following are recommended for consideration when looking critically at one's class with a view to making improvements.

1 *Team work* Folk dance involves separate teams when danced in sets, and the whole class as a team in circle dances.

Every member of the group or circle is important, even when they are not dancing. Those waiting to join the dance must think ahead, ready to move in to start the next figure on the first bar of the music. Equally important, they must end a figure early enough to be in position for the next part of the dance. For example, in circling back to right after circling to left, the team must break their circle at count 7 to be back in own places on count 8 – not rushing back, late, after keeping hands joined for all eight counts.

Good team work also means keeping circles round, lines straight, sets rectangular, and keeping the correct distances between dancers in their team positions. After falling back to a set shape from circling or wheeling, all team members need to check their positions. In promenading round, side by side, in a big circle, all couples need to think about positions as well as neat footwork.

2 *Phrasing* Good phrasing means fitting the figures of a dance to the phrases of its music and being in the right place at the right time. Bad phrasing means arriving in position early and having to stand still, not dancing, or arriving late and having to rush into the next figure.

Dancers should start each figure on the first beat of its phrase of music, and carefully adjust their dancing so that they finish the figure on the last beat of that phrase of music. Perfect phrasing creates a smooth, flowing impression of dancers passing straight into a figure from the previous one, without any stops or starts in between.

3 *Footwork and technique* Every traditional dance lesson starts with footwork as a warm-up, and to develop quiet, neat, controlled footwork which is good enough to produce dance true to the traditions of the nation concerned.

Good technique refers to the quality of the steps – good footwork and its correct usage in performing the figures. To adapt the travelling, skip change of step in Scottish country dancing, for example, as you travel forward, backward, round in a wheel, longer to travel all round a figure-of-eight, or shorter when a slower change is needed, is to adapt good footwork to demonstrate good technique.

4 *General impression* There should be an impression of:

a enjoyment on the dancers' faces as they join in enthusiastically, both when dancing and when waiting their turn

b poised, upright carriage as they all try to look their best

c good use of hands to receive, assist, guide or to change places.

Reception Dance programme

AUTUMN	SPRING	SUMMER
1 Listen to the teacher, then respond quietly and quickly.	1 Work hard, almost without stopping, to improve and remember skills.	1 Work with increasing skill and confidence, expressed in neat, quiet, poised performances.
2 Improve basic travelling actions – walk, run, jump, hop, skip, bounce, slide, gallop.	2 Respond to rhythmic accompaniment, keeping in time with the music.	2 Be keen to practise, almost non-stop, until asked to stop and change to a new activity.
3 Use whole body movements thoughtfully to experience the varied actions possible.	3 Develop poise, control and good balance in travelling, jumping, landing, stillness and whole body stretching and bending.	3 Be aware of the importance of good poise and clear body shapes in enhancing a performance.
4 Use whole body movements wholeheartedly, using joints and muscles to their limit.	4 Respond rhythmically to set tasks, with short, repeating patterns and sequences of movement.	4 Be aware of the importance of good use of own space and whole room in adding variety and contrast to the work, and making space for others sharing the hall with you.
5 Use movements in isolated parts of the body, focusing on ways in which each can perform – feet, hands, arms, legs, back, head and shoulders.	5 Use body parts in a variety of ways to add contrast and interest – different shape, direction, size, speed and effort.	5 Practise simple, traditional dance steps and figures and use them in simple circle dances where all can see and copy the teacher.
6 Respond to varied stimuli – teacher, drum, music, poem, song, imagery: 'bubbles', 'ball', 'puppet', 'robot'.	6 Learn simple, traditional dance steps and figures and use them in simple, circle folk-style dances.	6 Learn to link a series of actions together, rhythmically, in a short, repeating pattern.
7 Watch with interest to learn from others.	7 Skip alone and with a partner, to folk dance music, feeling and keeping to the 8-count phrasing typical of this music.	7 Respond to varied stimuli – folk dance music, poem, song, imagery, nature, approaching holidays.
8 Be body-shape aware, still and moving, using whole body in firm, poised posture.	8 Use imagery widely as a stimulus to actions – 'like a bubble, gently floating; slowly turning; sinking'.	8 Express feelings and ideas through body movement – the wonder of natural birth and growth in spring.
9 Share space well so that all can practise freely, understanding 'own space' and 'whole room space'.	9 Respond to varied stimuli – drum, music, poem, song, nursery rhyme, imagery, body contact sounds.	9 Link actions together neatly with a still start and finish, and a neat, well-planned middle.
10 Co-operate with a partner, leading, following, copying, combining, observing and commenting on their work.	10 Enjoy linking a series of simple actions and building them into an easily remembered, repeating pattern.	10 Co-operate with a partner, leading, following, observing, coaching.
11 Celebrate Christmas with a seasonal dance.	11 Watch a demonstration and be able to say what was pleasing and possibly worth copying.	11 Create a seasonal 'Holidays' dance.
		12 Be an interested and encouraging observer, with helpful comments.

Year 1

Dance programme

AUTUMN	SPRING	SUMMER
1 Dress correctly; behave well; listen and respond quickly.	1 Respond wholeheartedly with vigour.	1 Be aware of good spacing, able to change direction to avoid impeding others, and for safety.
2 Find out movements possible in isolated body parts – head, spine, arms, hands, feet, legs.	2 Share space safely and unselfishly.	2 Develop skill, always trying to improve, working alone and with a partner.
3 Use whole body movements to reach into all the space round self, still and travelling.	3 Neatly link actions together, with confidence and control.	3 Improve by making work neater, more varied, with changes of shape, direction, speed and effort.
4 Look for and travel to spaces, using and improving varied actions – walk, run, jump, skip, hop, bounce, slide, gallop.	4 Demonstrate skills, enhanced by using variety and contrasts.	4 Co-operate with a partner to decide how to plan to respond to a challenge wholeheartedly.
5 Co-operate with a partner, leading, following, copying.	5 Express ideas through movement, e.g. 'Winter' freezing streams and melting, dripping icicles.	5 Respond rhythmically to music and percussion to perform short patterns of movement that can be repeated and remembered.
6 Respond enthusiastically and with imagination to challenges.	6 Create rhythmic patterns of joined up movements that can be repeated.	6 Use contrasts, like variety, as a way of enhancing performance.
7 Celebrate autumn with e.g. 'Autumn Leaves' and their windy day movements.	7 Be able to demonstrate contrasts in use of speed, shape and tension.	7 Perform dances with a poised start and finish, and a smooth, neatly linked-up middle.
8 Use vocal sounds to accompany e.g. 'Leaves' and 'Fireworks' dances.	8 Understand nature of 'Opposites' – heavy, light, strong, gentle – and express them in a partner dance.	8 Express nature's seasonal period of growth and birth through bodily movement.
9 Learn traditional dance steps and figures. Combine them in a four-part pattern in a simple set made up of single couples.	9 Learn simple movements and figures of traditional dance and use them with a partner.	9 Use vocal sounds rhythmically as stimuli to inspire and accompany movements.
10 Celebrate 'Christmas' with e.g. 'Fairy in the Toyshop' and the clowns, robots and penguins being brought into action, one at a time, by the fairy's wand.	10 Respond to varied stimuli – music, objects and imagery, winter words, partners, opposites.	10 Express moods and feelings by body movement and develop into a dance with a partner, 'Making a little pattern you can remember and repeat.'
11 Enjoy performing and observing, learning from own and others' comments on good quality work.	11 Continue to develop control and co-ordination in basic ations such as travelling, jumping, stillness and gesture.	11 Become a keen, appreciative observer of others' movement, keen, also, to learn from others.
	12 Be keen to practise, repeat, improve, remember and present a performance.	
	13 Try to 'feel' movement quality contrasts as in light, gentle travelling bubbles, and the hard, jagged frozen stream.	
	14 Be an interested spectator, and be encouraging by making helpful comments.	

Year 2

Dance programme

AUTUMN	SPRING	SUMMER

AUTUMN

1 Dress safely and sensibly.
2 Respond readily and quickly to instructions. Keep practising.
3 Improve basic actions by adding clear shapes and good poise.
4 Work hard to make the lessons 'Scenes of busy activity'.
5 Become body parts aware – feet, ankles, legs, hands, arms, shoulders, and link actions in short, repeating patterns.
6 Experience working with range of stimuli – actions, body parts, fireworks, music, poems, partners, Christmas.
7 Demonstrate ability to plan and perform a series of joined up actions, neatly.
8 Link these movements with increasing control by using changes of direction, level, speed and tension.
9 Demonstrate knowledge and understanding through actions.
10 Celebrate 'Fireworks' with good use of shape, speed, effort and direction as in rockets, Catherine wheels and bangers.
11 Celebrate Christmas with 'Puppet Makers', making a simple story, expressing the weary maker, the happy puppets and the excitement of the chase.
12 Describe what they and others have done and how they did it.

SPRING

1 Perform simple, basic actions such as travelling, jumping, turning and stillness, with positive, confident, correct, poised use of the body.
2 Experience and be guided in making dances with clear beginnings, middles and ends.
3 Demonstrate increasing control over use of shape, space and effort.
4 Plan a 'Winter' dance with a partner and percussion, based on three, seasonal, winter words on a card.
5 Demonstrate how good use of contrasts enhances a dance, as in winter's 'Freeze' and 'Melt'.
6 Co-operate with a partner, often observing, commenting and, sometimes, suggesting how to improve a performance.
7 Learn traditional dance steps and figures, and simple international circle dances, where class can see teacher.
8 Create simple characters and little stories in response to music. Explore feelings.
9 Describe simple actions seen, using simple terms to describe.

SUMMER

1 Demonstrate good body control in travelling, jumping and stillness.
2 Demonstrate an enthusiasm and ability to practise to improve.
3 Respond rhythmically to music with skill, poise, balance and co-ordination.
4 Be given opportunities to explore moods and feelings through structured tasks.
5 Create simple characters, expressing them through their body movements.
6 Work often with a partner to improve and extend the skills learned and to share in creating something bigger than can be achieved alone.
7 Link movements to demonstrate an understanding of the elements of 'movement' – shape, space, effort, speed.
8 Make a seasonal 'Nature' dance to show how animals or plants come into being. Kittens or lambs are examples of well-known stimuli, inspiring lively action.
9 Demonstrate knowledge and understanding mainly through physical actions rather than verbal expression.
10 Learn and perform a simple, traditional, British circle dance, and revise other folk dances learned previously.
11 Work harder for longer with greater confidence, control and versatility.
12 Express moods and feelings in a three-part dance about infant school days – shy start; good middle; brilliant end.
13 Make simple, friendly judgements on how others have performed.

Year 3

Dance programme

AUTUMN	SPRING	SUMMER

AUTUMN

1 Listen and respond immediately to instructions. Use neat, quiet actions.
2 Dress sensibly and safely. Share floor space unselfishly and safely.
3 Work wholeheartedly, practising varied basic travelling actions and linking them into repeating patterns in time with music.
4 Develop awareness of basic actions and of how body parts concerned are working – feet, legs, hands and trunk.
5 Compose steps, hands and whole body patterns and be able to repeat them.
6 Become body shape aware. Understand how clear, firm shapes enhance the look of basic actions.
7 Celebrate the seasonal 'Fireworks' with their varied starting shapes, contrasting actions and varied use of body tension and speed.
8 Plan and link skills and work hard to practise and improve them.
9 Celebrate Christmas in the 'Puppet Maker's Workshop', and experience the jerky, floppy, loose movements of puppets – plus the movements of their sad maker.
10 Observe demonstrations by partner and others and make helpful comments about what was admired.

SPRING

1 Plan short, expressive performance based on winter words on cards, contrasting e.g. the rushing stream with the floating snowflake and spiky ice shapes with melting snow.
2 Develop skill in basic travelling actions, keeping the rhythm of accompanying music.
3 Learn, and join creatively, folk dance figures, for couples.
4 Practise to improve, remember and be able to repeat patterns of movement.
5 Learn a simple, traditional, folk dance, co-operating with a partner and a team, learning about the good quality features involved.
6 Use body contact rhythmic sounds as a dance accompaniment and stimulus.
7 Experience and be praised for planning and creating a dance.
8 Enrich movements by understanding and varying shape, direction, speed, level and body tension.
9 Express identity of characters through body movements they use. Plan and practise repeating patterns of circus work actions.
10 Recognise and describe a set of movement patterns.

SUMMER

1 Make dances with clear beginnings, middles and ends.
2 Be given opportunities to work alone to develop own personal skill.
3 Be given opportunities to work with a partner to share ideas and combine to make a bigger, more special dance.
4 Learn an easy, traditional, circle dance, listening and responding to the rhythm of the accompanying music.
5 Compose and control movements by varying speed and tension. Develop in a partners 'Fast and Slow' dance.
6 Experience working with a variety of stimuli, including music.
7 Express moods, ideas and feelings imaginatively through the body actions usually associated with them.
8 Display increasing self-confidence, control and versatility, enthusiastically practising to improve and share achievements.
9 Comment on what they and others have just shown.

Year 4 — Dance programme

AUTUMN	SPRING	SUMMER
1 Respond readily; dress well; and practise wholeheartedly to improve a performance.	1 Enrich movements by varying shape, space, direction, speed and tension elements for variety and contrast.	1 Improve and refine content in dances with clear beginnings, middles and ends.
2 Increase complexity of basic actions, step patterns and varied uses of body parts.	2 Make rhythmic responses, through repeating patterns, to set tasks.	2 Work hard to develop own ideas and display independence of thought and action.
3 Respond to music, performing longer sequences, alone and with others.	3 Use winter action words on cards as immediate stimuli to seasonal action. Partners can use percussion accompaniment.	3 Be aware of good posture, always, and the correct use of the body when performing apparently simple actions.
4 Illustrate varied movement qualities, as in 'Autumn Leaves' use of space, shape, speed and tension.	4 Creatively link four figures from a selection of traditional dance figures with smooth flow and good teamwork, all in time with music.	4 Show control, poise and expression in use of gestures to demonstrate ideas, feelings and moods.
5 Use vocal sounds to accompany and inspire actions, alone and with a partner.	5 Create characters by expressing them through the bodily movements associated with them.	5 Learn a simple, international folk dance to improve class repertoire. Be able to improve, remember and repeat the dance, illustrating and describing its main features.
6 Make up dances with clear start, middle and ending.	6 Be able to repeat a series of movements remembered over a period of time.	6 Contribute fully to partner and group activity, as a good listener and good planner, able to see ahead to the intended outcome.
7 Working with a partner, listen to, share and develop ideas.	7 Demonstrate a capacity for originality and an enthusiasm for using and presenting it.	7 Accompany 'Our Class Machine' dance with vocal sounds to inspire slow, quick, smooth, jerky, soft, heavy, straight and circular movements.
8 Experience different pathways and shapes, leading and following a partner to use them.	8 Make simple judgements about own and others' performances, and suggest ways to improve.	8 Exude vigour, poise, control, variety and contrast and an impression that 'This is easy.'
9 Repeat, improve and remember longer sequences of repeating patterns of movement.	9 Be found 'Working, not waiting; practising, not watching; and giving an impression of wholehearted participation,' at all times.	9 Be able to comment on a contrast in a pattern of movement.
10 Celebrate Christmas in a 'Snow Dance' with its combination of teacher-led and pupil created patterns.		
11 Describe when elements of a dance are well performed.		

Year 5

Dance programme

AUTUMN	SPRING	SUMMER

AUTUMN

1 Practise to develop basic skills of travelling, jumping, turning and gesture by linking them together in increasingly complex sequences.

2 Tackle more complex tasks with enthusiasm and inventiveness.

3 Be assisted and encouraged to plan, refine and adapt performance when working alone or with others.

4 Show how variety and contrast enhance a performance in a partner's 'Opposites' dance, with changing actions, speeds, effort, shape, direction or level.

5 Use repeating patterns of movement to enable sequences to be remembered with increasing control and accuracy

6 Improve the effect of a performance by including moments of stillness within a pattern.

7 Use action words on cards to inspire actions; with partners commenting for an improvement; and partner's percussion providing the rhythm.

8 Create a simple story, e.g. 'Jaws', expressing ideas through whole body movement.

9 Observe and describe the expressive features of dance.

SPRING

1 Plan, perform and appraise longer sequences of movement.

2 Recognise the need for physical competence in stillness and in movement.

3 Use winter words on cards as an immediate stimulus to movement, with basic 'Scatter' of the snowflakes being expressed in different ways, using varied qualities, speeds, shapes and tensions.

4 Demonstrate versatile, whole body movement, able to focus on spine, arms, shoulders as well as legs.

5 Create a traditional-style folk dance using four of seven figures taught in a circle. Co-operate with three other couples to agree the four, repeating figures.

6 Learn an English set dance as a contrast to the created circle dance.

7 Repeat a series of movements performed previously. A 'Favourite Dance' can be requested.

8 Plan imaginatively to contrast a partner's actions. 'Anything you can do, I can do different!'

9 Explain own couple's contrasts and point out those of other couples.

SUMMER

1 Contribute fully to partner and group activity, mixing well and being considerate towards others' ideas.

2 Express ideas, moods, feelings, and create a simple story in movement, e.g. 'Small Beginnings' as the mountain stream rushes, bubbles, twists and wells into a wide river.

3 Learn an international folk dance, e.g. 'Simi Yadech' of Israel, to expand class repertoire, and to inspire almost non-stop, vigorous activity.

4 Work in a group to plan and create a dance based on 'Feelings'.

5 With a partner, use voice sounds as an accompaniment to observed movement, and in groups using voice sound as an accompaniment to words describing holiday places, activities or foods.

6 Display capacity for vigorous, but neat, wholehearted, but poised, thoughtful, well-planned practising and performing.

7 Be taught to help selves to improve by making simple judgements on performances.

Year 6 — Dance programme

AUTUMN	SPRING	SUMMER
1 Perform dance steps with skill, accuracy and increased poise.	1 Repeat sequences with increasing control and accuracy.	1 Move with increased poise, control and co-ordination.
2 Perform more complex patterns of movement, neatly linked, with interesting use of shapes, speed, directions and effort.	2 Compose and control movements by varying shape, direction, speed and effort.	2 Be able to improve, repeat and remember a dance, focusing on one main movement feature at a time.
3 Work habitually at maximum effort, taking muscles and joints to their fullest use – with much deep breathing and perspiration.	3 Be able to lead, follow, mirror and copy a partner's movements exactly.	3 Make short dances with clear beginnings, middles and ends.
4 Plan, compose and present short dances with an understanding of elements of 'Style' – variety, contrasts, and skilful movement.	4 Perform compositions created by self and others with good form, style and clear technical demands.	4 Express feelings, moods and ideas and create simple characters and stories in response to a range of stimuli, as in 'Good Samaritan'.
5 Accompany short sequences with vocal accompaniment to stimulate contrasting actions.	5 Express 'Winter' in movement, responding to seasonal words, percussion, and help from an observing partner.	5 Learn and perform a folk dance from outside the British Isles, e.g. a less vigorous, more relaxed and gesture-filled Caribbean dance.
6 Respond imaginatively to varied challenges and stimuli, showing increasing skill, versatility and an awareness of 'movement'.	6 Be whole body conscious in expressing movement qualities, in a 'larger than life' way.	6 Work in groups to plan, practise and remember longer dances in response to varied stimuli. Such dances often include a teacher-directed start and finish, and a group created middle, as in 'In The Mood' and 'Rock 'N Roll'.
7 Create a seasonal autumn dance such as 'Autumn Trees', with a vocal accompaniment to varied movement qualities in trunk, branches and leaves.	7 Plan and perform own traditional style dance, using four of the figures taught, in a 32-bar, repeating dance.	7 Work wholeheartedly and with enthusiasm, increasingly stamping performances with own special style and personality.
8 Show ability to recognise, then pass on a movement to another, emphasising clearly its main features.	8 Learn, improve and remember a well-known, popular, British Isles folk dance.	8 Give an impression of confidence and concentration, always trying to improve and achieve.
9 Make well-informed comments on another's work and indicate how to improve it.	9 Be physically active for own sake; mindful of others for their sake; and proud of good footwork and good teamwork in folk dance.	9 Observe a performance, pick out good quality features, and make helpful, encouraging comments.
	10 Express moods and ideas and create simple characters in a story like 'City Life'.	
	11 Compare two performances and indicate differences in content and effectiveness.	

Index